New Methods in
Social Science Research

New Methods in Social Science Research

Policy Sciences and Futures Research

T. Harrell Allen

OCT 2 8 1980

PRAEGER

PRAEGER SPECIAL STUDIES • PRAEGER SCIENTIFIC

Library of Congress Cataloging in Publication Data

Allen, T. Harrell.
  New methods in social science research.

  Includes bibliographies.
  1. Social sciences—Methodology. 2. Policy sciences.
3. Social policy. I. Title.
H62.A4575   300'.1'8   76-12840
ISBN 0-275-23630-7

PRAEGER SPECIAL STUDIES
200 Park Avenue, New York, N.Y., 10017, U.S.A.

Published in the United States of America in 1978
by Praeger Publishers,
A Division of Holt, Rinehart and Winston, CBS, Inc.

9 038 98765432

©1978 by Praeger Publishers

Printed in the United States of America

Another one for Maston and Carol

Preface

This book was written at full throttle. Today's social problems, because of their complexity and urgency, leave little lead time for developing solutions, or as Lord Ashby said, "There is no guaranteed tenure for man on Earth." If we must operate in the short run, then much will depend on the policies we implement for coping with poverty, crime, pollution, energy, and ecology, for they allow us an opportunity to extend human survival and tenure. Erroneous policies will result in nothing more than well-meaning failure. All too often our attempts to solve complex, counterintuitive social problems can be likened to a group of people lost in the woods in a thick fog. They can't see the forest for the trees.

The aim of this book is to help solve social problems through better policy making that results from new advances in social science methodology. My philosophy is grounded in a belief that academic knowledge can and must be relevant to real-world problems. A behavioral outcome of this philosophy has been this book. One of the goals of this book is to foster a respect for intellectual achievement along with an appreciation of its relationship to good common sense. Usually this means perceiving a problem, adequately describing it, thinking it through. To do this requires a certain level of cognitive and theoretical apparatus. The chapters of this book are intended to be such an apparatus.

The book has been written for two principal audiences: For those academicians who are interested in applying their knowledge and training to the solution of social problems, and for those beleagured policy makers who must make crucial decisions regardless of whether they get any help from the first group. The book is very concerned with improving the policy-making process. Having worked in both camps I believe each group has much to learn from the other, and I also believe this can be done while maintaining the integrity of the intellectual effort.

Since I am well aware of the pragmatic question, "What do we do on Monday morning?" I believe the book will be useful to such policy makers as planners, systems analysts, economists, managers and administrators, environmentalists, budget analysts, and applied social and behavioral scientists. I hope this book will serve as something of a Rorschach test: Different readers will come up with different uses of it.

A basic premise of the book is that there have been advances in social science knowledge that can be extremely applicable to complex social problems. Such knowledge is more of a methodological nature than a new discovery of factual data. To understand and come to grips with today's problems will require novel uses of science. Much of the dogma that surrounds the methodology of the scientific method will have to be cast aside if we are to make progress in solving social ills. That this will not be easy is one of the more humbling experiences in writing this book.

Ever since the publication in 1685 of his treatise <u>De Motu</u>, the laws of Sir Isaac Newton have been as much a liability as an asset. In one law that has been especially troublesome, he warned us that to every action there must be an equal and opposite reaction, and the nation's social scientists have believed him. Whenever some original thinker has tried to push the pendulum of received opinion one way, all the custodians of established dogma have rushed to swing it back in the opposite direction. The result is that today, after nearly a century of social science mechanics, our methodological machinery is not what it could be, but rather what it always was.

In essence, this book calls for a Copernican revolution in the social sciences. Society must again become "the center" about which social science revolves, rather than social science research at the center. The book is not so much ground-breaking as it hopefully is ground-establishing in the sense that it brings together under one cover ideas that have been advanced by insightful thinkers.

The first three chapters lay the necessary philosophical groundwork for embarking on novel approaches to social science methodology. These chapters identify the critical methodological perspective that must be acquired if the social science disciplines are to analyze social problems successfully.

The second half of the book is devoted to spelling out the new methodologies for accomplishing effective policy making. The book has been organized in such a way that it is usable for theoretical advance as well as for practical application.

Throughout the book the male pronouns "he" or "his" are used. This is a matter of style rather than oversight; I have always attempted to practice liberation. I have given in to convention and used the male gender simply because I think "he or she" phrasing produces such awkward sentence structure.

Finally a personal note, although I usually regard such comments to be an intrusion of privacy. I want to thank M and C for granting me the time that is really theirs to write this book.

Contents

LIST OF FIGURES

New Methods in
Social Science Research

1

The Need for New Methodology

At 5:17 p.m. in Buffalo, 5:17 in Rochester, 5:18 in Boston, 5:28 in Albany, 5:24 to 5:28 in New York City, the clocks in the Megalopolis stopped. Lights blinked and dimmed and went out. Skyscrapers stood like black monoliths against a cold November sky lit only by the moon. Subways ground dead in their tunnels. Streetcars froze in their tracks. Street lights and traffic signals went out. Elevators hung immobile in their shafts. Airports shut down. Computers lost their memories. Television pictures darkened and died. Business stopped. Nothing seemed to work except transistor radios, and finally this communication medium delivered the news that the world had not come to an end, Armageddon had not occurred, but that almost the entire Northeast was darkened by the most colossal power failure in history.

The northeastern Megalopolis—a vast intermeshing of cities, towns, and suburbs—is urban America of the late twentieth century brought to its fullest flower, and its fullest fragility.

On November 9, 1965, the Megalopolis fell victim to its very dependence on "the system." The system, in this case, was the sprawling, interconnected grid of power networks that girdle the region. A system that depends on turbine technology and runs on an electrical metabolism and operates on a blind faith that one has only to push a button or flick a switch to make it work. And when the electricity stopped so did the system. It was a blackout or breakdown that was not supposed to have happened. Only a year before, a Federal Power Commission report had pronounced such grids relatively invulnerable even to nuclear attack.

At its peak the power failure was simply beyond human scale: Like a string of Christmas-tree lights, one power system after another blinked out in a wave of failures cascading down from the upper reaches

1

of the grid in Ontario, Canada, sweeping across upstate New York, racing across most of New England, dimming lights momentarily as far north as Maine and as far south as Washington. It engulfed 80,000 square miles across parts of eight states and left 30 million people in the dark. In all the Megalopolis, New York City had the longest blackout, more than 13 hours in some parts, and the worst problems because of its density in population. It affected the most people: 600,000 trapped in stalled subways, nearly 100,000 stranded waiting for commuter trains, numberless hundreds caged in elevators, and numberless thousands trapped in skyscrapers like primitive cliff dwellers—only worse, because unlike the ancients they could not get down. And New York's recovery was the slowest, taking almost two days for the city to return to normal.

Incredibly, the blackout stopped short of catastrophe. There were no plane crashes despite airport lights' going out, no train wrecks, no disastrous fires, no crime waves, and no panic. Yet it did have for moments that turned into hours the quality of a science fiction thriller; it was the night when, to all appearances, the world stood still.

Thus the power failure that the experts said could not happen did and the immediate cause remained elusive for days afterward.

The power-line grid connecting the 23 electric utility companies of the Northeast is like a safety rope linking mountain climbers. It is designed to support a faltering member, but then something happened and it yanked all the others down. The common bond became a common snare and caused the biggest power failure in history.

At 5:15 p.m. Tuesday, the power network was in perfect balance. Then the delicate power system began to go haywire. The first sign of the coming systemic breakdown was a large increase in power flow to the east and south. The flow to New York, for example, jumped to 490,000 kilowatts. At Con Edison there was a quick drop in frequency. This meant that somewhere in the system something was putting generators of incoming alternating current out of step, and they were in turn literally fighting other generators. For Con Ed and for all companies experiencing similar signals, it was time to cut loose from the network. But there was no chance to bail out. The chain reaction had started with direction reversals of load, loss of synchronization among utility units, and automatic shutdown of generators. All of this took place in only four seconds. Operators never had a chance to reach the console controls to cut loose manually. All they could do was watch as safety switches cut off their own local generators to keep them from being overloaded and damaged. Additional breakdowns occurred and in about 12 minutes all generators stopped. And in a twist of systemic irony, no one can be quite sure of the exact time, since electric clocks depend for their accuracy on a constant flow of electricity at precisely 60 cycles per second, and with flickering current that was impossible.

No one is certain what caused this massive power failure. It would appear that a circuit breaker in Ontario tripped, power then shifted to other lines overloading them, and they in turn tripped. Consequently a single power-limit pullout triggered a chain reaction of power failures. But a single cause for the failure has not been established: no severed transmission line, no defective generator, no faulty circuit breaker has been found. In fact, the automatic equipment functioned without error. Engineers are inclined to blame the laws of probability. A series of "instabilities" or flickers in the grid combined in a fantastically improbable sequence to bring the whole network down. By all odds it could not happen. But it did.

SYSTEMIC BREAKDOWN

I have used this lengthy example because it is a real-world illustration of systems failure. The massive power failure demonstrates both the potency and impotence of open or real-world systems. The power of the network grid as an electrical generating system is obvious, and what was not so obvious before the 1965 failure is the fragility of the system. The blackout underscored the fact that system integration is often taken for granted or poorly understood. Each utility company was a component in the bigger system, the network grid, but each had different capacities of power generation and load and regulating methods. All lumped together, the big system was designed to handle single, large-scale problems, but not combinations of simultaneous disturbances within the system. Being a goal-directed system, the backup relay had been set at a particular capacity in 1963. But subsequent power flows in 1965 had changed and apparently on Tuesday, November 9, 1965, the power flow exceeded the level at which the relay was set and the circuit breaker tripped out the line. The equipment performed as it was designed to do with the result that the entire power system began to function as a positive feedback loop. In short, things were out of control with deviation being amplified.

Power systems are designed to protect the system against loss of power generation and not against massive blocks of power load. What happened in 1965 illustrates how vulnerable complex systems may be to abnormal occurrences.

The power failure (actually the equipment performed perfectly) also dramatized the need for human control of automatic systems. Apparently most of the operating personnel were not aware of the 1963 relay setting, nor had there been any planning for unusual contingencies or improbable events.

Finally the power system failure realistically demonstrated the high interdependency between systems in a technological society. The subsequent effects dramatize the interface between the power system and the system of towns and cities in the Northeast. What was so well demonstrated on that cold November night was the systemic principle that to disturb one component in a system will in some way disturb the other components. We can also see in those events of 1965 that no system operates independently of other supra- and subsystems. The failure of the power system caused the whole transportation system of New York City to fail. In addition, restoration of power took many hours because each utility company had to throw its own switches, check its own relays, start its own generators, and synchronize its own frequencies with other companies (components), otherwise the entire system might throw itself off again.

This real-world example of system failure dramatizes the need for methodology that is sensitive to systemic relationships, recognizes the need for handling holistic systems, and can plan for appropriate procedures for meeting contingencies.

SOCIAL SYSTEMS BREAKDOWN

Talk with any thinking individual and he or she can cite a long list of social problems that need immediate attention. Many of these have affected the person's quality of life in a direct way. Typically the concerned citizen is anxious to see someone, industry or government, solve them. Additionally he cannot understand why "science" or "technology" cannot produce solutions for these unsolved problems. Certainly he is correct in believing that such urban problems as pollution, mass transit systems, crime prevention, adequate health care facilities, traffic jams, and congested airports have technological aspects to their origins and solutions. He is justified in asking: If NASA can provide clean air for astronauts in outer space then why smog in Los Angeles? Why must one allow an hour for getting to the airport when the flight will take only 25 minutes? Why does the freeway jam when there are no accidents and there is an express lane for buses? Such problems have now reached such proportions that the individual trying to cope with them can only throw his hands up in anguish and mutter, "Nothing works anymore."

However, it would be as simple as it would be misleading to state that all of the foregoing are products of a technological age and can be solved through technology. Such an answer would fail to recognize that the modern way of life has produced a global village in which people are forced to live together without knowing how or being aware of the interdependencies between man, machine, and environment.

Actually, many of our problems are not so much technological ones as they reflect man's failure to provide adequate social change along with technological advances—a philosophical paradox of technical progress with planning primitivism. For example, we have now created a gene in a test tube reflecting our understanding of the basic secrets of the life process, while at the same time we cannot handle a simple biological problem of population explosion. And the computer age shows that we have learned to extend our brains electronically, but anyone who has attempted to correct an error on a computerized bill is aware that while we use the computer it is quite easy to be used by it.

One senses a mood of irritation among the citizenry as problems seem to defy the "experts." There seems to be a growing lack of patience with those who are supposed to know. Answers are too slow in coming, and compared with the need they fall far short. Many of our social problems are large and complex and some are so severe that disaster threatens. All of us realize that the failure to solve our societal problems may actually be an acceleration toward disaster. Because of this we do not have the lead time to stop and start over many times, because we headed in grossly wrong directions when looking for solutions. There is no time to follow intellectual cul-de-sacs.

THE FAILURE OF SOCIAL SCIENCE

A closer examination of the current problems reveals that rather than being technological, they are complex combinations of social, cultural, economic, psychological, legal, and communications factors. In short, "human" problems. This means that social and behavioral scientists must bear much of the responsibility for generating solutions to our problems. One would expect to find such solutions resulting from social science research. Unfortunately, much of the research has had very little effect on real-world problems. The social science record of accomplishment when dealing with applied research has not been impressive, especially considering the number of social scientists. The emphasis has been on selecting problems whose solutions are presently available rather than attempting to solve novel problems. As Kuhn (1962) has observed, the scientific community tends to encourage its members to undertake only those problems that have known solutions.

The report of the Special Commission on the Social Sciences of the National Science Board (1969) is hard-pressed to provide vivid illustrations in which findings have led to the solution of social problems and action.

Here are some specific reasons for the failure of the social sciences in solving large-scale social problems such as poverty, racial conflicts, and violence.

Exclusive reliance on a reductionist philosophy of science. Social scientists have followed physics and chemistry as pure models of how to conduct "scientific" research. The slant of these disciplines has been largely analytic, with the whole being reduced to smaller parts; molecules to atoms; atoms into smaller particles, and so on. Using this approach the whole became the sum of its parts.

Overemphasis on causality. This has led to seeing any problem reduced to independent and dependent variables, stimulus-response paradigms, cause and effect relationships, while failing to realize that most living systems are probabilistic or stochastic rather than deterministic.

A failure to realize that social problems must be viewed as holistic problems or systems. That is, they cannot be reduced to components that are separable. In fact, whole systems components are nonseparable and cannot be measured or evaluated apart from the whole system of which they are a part. In short, the whole is greater than the sum of its parts. For example, a problem like energy, poverty, or urban decay cannot be reduced to a few simple causes, because its components are buried in such other systems as economics, culture, race, education, and law. One cannot attack part of the problem, one must attack the whole problem if progress is to be made.

An error in self-perception that the practice of science is "value-free" and more basic than applied. Certainly anyone familiar with the history of science knows that it is not free of prejudice and it is practiced by human beings full of frailty. Galileo wrote his ideas in code because he was afraid someone would steal them; Newton as president of the Royal Society appointed a committee of friends to declare that he, rather than Leibniz, was the inventor of the calculus; and James Watson's race for the Nobel Prize as told in his The Double Helix all suggest that contemporary science is vulnerable to feuds, secrecy, paranoia, and jealousy. Nevertheless the myth that physical science—all science, in fact—is value-free and that only pure research is basic has led many social scientists to shy away from applied research.

Applied social science as only a marginal part of the scholarly literature. With the emphasis in academia on "publish or perish" and in particular on the younger Ph. D. s, then social scientists must write for professional journals rather than attempting to solve society's problems.

Social science research findings that are fragmented, overspecialized, and method-centered. In spite of sophisticated designs, data manipulation, higher mathematics, most research findings are useless and unrelated to previous findings. In short, there is a definite lack of integration of the findings and no real-world application. To use the jargon, such research lacks external validity.

A lack of theory to guide social science research into the problem-solving area. The kind of theory needed for understanding complex social problems is vastly different from that of most laboratory research. Real-world problems require the social scientist to leave such comforts as laboratory controls, no time constraints, perfectionism, models, and precise measurement and quantification. Rather than viewing this with alarm he should realize that such demands reflect misapplications of physical science, and that the world will have to deal with its problems regardless of whether it gets any help from us.

A lack of communication (even technical) between social scientists and their disciplines. Research findings relevant to another discipline are not exchanged, and with the growing use of technical jargon it is not clear that they would be understood if communicated.

METHODOLOGICAL FOUNDATIONS

From the above criticisms it is obvious that much of the failure of social science research to solve or even attack societal problems is due to a misorientation of methodological stance.

"Methodology" is a term much misused by current social scientists. It has become a phrase or synonym for "method" or "technique." As Blumer (1969) noted, "Today, 'methodology' is regarded with depressing frequency as synonymous with the study of procedures, and a 'methodologist' is one who is expertly versed in the knowledge and use of such procedures."

Actually the term methodology has an even more important epistemological meaning concerned with the role of theory in research efforts. In this role, methodology functions like theory, as Kaplan (1964) points out, in guiding the conduct of inquiry. All science begins in philosophy, and, hence, methodology has a philosophical base that is oriented toward techniques and ways of knowing. Thus methodology becomes first an approach toward inquiry and then later evolves into particular methods or techniques. So today the word methodology can be used in two different but overlapping ways, the applied and the theoretical. In the applied usage one is mainly concerned with selecting specific technical tools and techniques for collecting data and analyzing it. In the theoretical usage one is chiefly concerned with philosophical fields of inquiry that can be used to conceptualize the problem under study. This book is mainly concerned with the theoretical usage, because the methodological choices made concerning the ap-plied have to be made after judgments have been made concerning the proper approaches to use. Such judgments are essentially ways of conceptualizing.

It is my basic theme that much of social science methodology is not adapted to interpreting how social systems behave. This is true for two reasons. First, social science research has adopted only one usage for methodology, the narrow selection of methods and tools, while ignoring the conceptualization role of methodology. This leads to mistaken "scientific" practices. Second, our social systems be-long to the class of problems described by Forrester (1961) as "multi-loop nonlinear feedback systems." Much of the social science meth-odology of today does not have the proper methodological foundation to interpret the dynamic behavior of our social systems. As a result the system that has been described by traditional social science meth-odology does not behave the way the social scientist expected it to. Because of system dynamics, applied methodology leads us face to face with the counterintuitive behavior of social systems.

Multiloop nonlinear feedback systems are counterintuitive in their behaviors because such systems are more complex and interde-pendent than our technological systems. The dynamic consequences of social systems are much more difficult to intuit than those of me-chanical systems. Such difficulty is somewhat due to the inability of the human mind to store such complex relationships, and some of it stems from methodological perspectives that focus on structure rather than implied behavior.

Real-world evidence of expected behavior differing from actual behavior is easily seen in our social problems. It may be useful to state several observations concerning social systems that lead to wrong predictions.

First, most policies aimed at changing the behavior of a system fail because most complex social systems are remarkably resilient to outside efforts of change. Much of this is due to successful change efforts on much simpler systems, such as mechanical systems, which are then applied to a vastly different and more complex system, like poverty or higher education. Or another source of error springs from a premature identification of symptom as cause, again resulting from an erroneous isomorphic identification of a simple system with a more complex one.

Second, social systems seem to have few points of leverage where the behavior of the system can be altered. The identification of such pressure points is crucial if one is going to be successful in altering the system's behavior. Failure to find these points of influ-ence will force the would-be change agent to repeat the French prov-erb, "The more things change the more they stay the same."

Third, short-term efforts at changing the system often run counter to long-term goals. There is a tendency to deal with the immediate or short-term problems of the system, but this may actually result in greater problems for the system in the long run. Many of our social systems are in trouble today because only short-term problems were dealt with years ago.

HOLISTIC METHODOLOGY

It is important early on to draw a clear distinction between a methodology that is oriented toward gathering and testing data and a methodology that is philosophically committed to serve as a guide to action. The first is concerned with building up the body of knowledge in an area or discipline and constructing theory. The second is primarily concerned with providing information relevant to a policy decision that must be made. Or, as Coleman (1972) distinguishes the two methodological stances: "discipline research," designed to advance knowledge in a scientific discipline and "policy research," designed to serve as a guide to social action. Obviously a most fundamental philosophical difference exists between the two methodologies.

Historically, social science has been lacking in methodological groundings for experimenting with large social systems—or whole systems. Part of the reason social science has had so little effect in predicting or solving such social problems as poverty, violence, race, and pollution has been the absence of such a methodology for researching whole systems. It is argued here that the methodology for analyzing whole systems is vastly different in both philosophy and techniques from the methodology for the analysis of mechanistic systems. By whole systems I simply mean a system whose components are nonseparable. A system that cannot be reduced to the sum of its parts. Such a whole system, like the environment or world economy, cannot be analyzed in parts but must be understood as a whole. If it is to be changed, then the whole system must be dealt with, otherwise only minor or ineffective change will occur. We are slowly beginning to see that the concepts of the theory of relativity can be applied to the social sphere.

Fortunately such a methodology for dealing with whole systems, holistic methodology, is beginning to emerge. Holistic methodology, with its orientation toward methods of inquiry rather than tools or techniques per se, is concerned with the basic conceptualization or definition of problems—especially nonlinear multifeedback loop systems requiring policy action. Holistic methodology does not begin, "given a system," as normal or traditional social science begins, "given a hypothesis," but actually begins by trying to define the components or parts of the nonseparable system. Essentially it begins conceptualizing the parts of the system, its boundaries, its interface with other systems, the feedback loops, and other supra- and subsystems to which it is connected.

It is important to remember here that systems are not products of nature but are actually mental creations. Certainly systems have their real-world or physical counterparts as a university is both a physical plant (buildings and grounds) and is also an "education system." Systems are also the abstract concepts of humans. If our social systems, while physically real, are also mental constructs, it is crucial in our understanding and manipulation of them that we be reasonably correct in conceptualizing about them.

But the reader immediately sees the problem. People will describe or conceptualize the same system differently. And here we get another insight as to why our social systems often behave counterintuitively. Holistic methodology, while not a panacea to this problem, is at least aware of different conceptualizations of the same system. Hence it is aware that the primary difficulty in dealing with whole or nonseparable systems is conceptualization. Such a methodology is at least not psychologically naive as has been much of previous social science research with its failure to realize the role of the experimenter in dealing with the problem.

Social scientists thus find themselves in something of a double bind. They are in the uncomfortable position of having to deal with counterintuitive systems, and at the same time must construct a "holistic" methodology that is in itself a counterintuitive system. The rest of this book is concerned with the problem of constructing such a methodology. The methodological chapters that follow are concerned with both the philosophical and technical aspects of methods-building. In short, they become methodological guidelines. In the real world of policy and action there is an urgent need for a holistic methodology. As Cowan (1951) has pointed out, "In dealing with systems that act as a whole, more and more of the control must be put into the plan or design of the experiment and less and less direct manipulation of the system or its parts is called for." Feyerabend (1965) has shown in his rather perceptive analysis how the dominance of any one scientific approach in any science can lead to the metaphysical stagnation of that science. The point is that holistic methodology allows for different fundamental designs for attacking and solving systemic problems. All of the following chapters presuppose the concept of equifinality.

CRISIS IN CONFIDENCE

As noted earlier, there is a growing public disenchantment with the efforts of social science to solve social problems. Nisbet

(1975) wrote in the <u>New York Times Magazine</u> that the social scientist is, in the view of some, "a combination ne'er-do-well and enemy of both nature and the human community," and in the view of many, "he is a man whose claims to special knowledge about social problems and their solution are no longer quite credible." The result for the social sciences has been a marked decline of prestige and a concomitant loss of public confidence in their claims to special insight into complicated problems.

An interesting parallel development has been the emergence of policy making as a field of research. Policy research is namely normative research about alternative ways of organizing and gathering information so that a decision maker can make the most intelligent choices. This trend is due to such technological innovations as computers and communications media, the exponential acceleration of change, and the propensity of social problems to endure rather than go away. What this development suggests to me is that policy research stock will increase in value, and social science will be asked to contribute to its market value. Whether it will or not remains to be seen.

Most of Nisbet's criticisms are well grounded and stem from the practice of traditional social science. As Lekachman (1976) puts it, "It is entirely wholesome that social scientists are now marked-down gurus, both because they deserve their fate and because adversity may guide them toward serious reconsideration of their tiresome pretensions to ethical neutrality and ideological purity."

Any discipline that calls itself a science will be judged and rewarded by its success in answering tough questions—such as society is demanding today. As Mayer (1976) correctly notes, politicians, educators, and bureaucrats have asked social scientists to propose policies, and when these policies were carried out—in slums, schools, hospitals, jails—the outcomes were wildly different from what had been predicted. Mayer concludes, "The vice of the social scientist is that unless somebody gives him a narrowly delimited target he will concentrate his efforts not on what is really happening but on what somebody else has written about it."

The tough questions still beg for answers. Can government be saved? Can a new energy source be found? Can television programs be based on some theme other than violence? Can cities be made safe places to live and work? Will bussing end racism? Are double-digit inflation and unemployment hopelessly intertwined? Such methodological tools as multivariate analysis are regarded by those outside the discipline as impotent in answering such questions. Policy makers have found the information produced by such methods failing to explain or predict human behavior—which are their primary concerns.

I do not know what the future will bring. I am not sure if social scientists will try to meet the societal problems head on and strive to

become philosopher-kings, or if they will hide in the academy and
find refuge from the realities of life. It is with some pessimism that
I detect signs of the latter. If most social scientists take this position, then I am afraid the party is over. Here are some reactions to
the criticisms of social science.

Loss of professional morale.
Retreat into more narrowly defined research under the innocuous
    label of "basic" research.
Return to strictly teaching activities.
Publication in professional literature (scholarly journals) of narrower
    and more specialized articles relative to broader approaches to
    problem solving.
Total divorce of social theory construction from empirical verifica-
    tion and model building.
Redoubling of "scientific" methods through the imitation of physical
    science methods of rigor, with none of the depth of understanding
    of the philosophy of science.

It is my hope that social scientists will not overreact to the
criticisms, however real and justified they may be. I do not think
that Nisbet was wrong in saying that social scientists have much to
answer for. There have been many successes and contributions by
social scientists in solving or contributing to the solution of tough social problems. In fact, some of these successes may have led the
public to expect too much too soon. As a result of some of this, the
public's conception of the social scientist has changed from that of a
dispassionate neutral observer to a participant in the social and political arena. I welcome that image because solving societal problems
is not a spectator sport.

As one who has done both "basic" and "applied" research, I am
aware that there is no clear "demilitarized zone" but more of a grey
overlapping area between the two activities. As one who has worked
in an R&D organization ("think-tank"), and a research-oriented university, I have seen basic research have very applied usage. So let
me emphasize to the reader that it is not my purpose here simply to
attack the social science discipline. I am stressing here the absence
of a methodology in the social sciences for a prescriptive, policy-
oriented study of social problems. Certainly, the social sciences
are not lacking in scientific methods and analysis. But the needs of
a prescriptive and policy-oriented methodology are quite different
from the needs of traditional social science methodology. The absence of such a methodology is the most basic reason for the inade-
quacies of most social sciences in solving complex social ills.

Neither is it suggested here that the development of a holistic
methodology will immediately produce answers for age-old problems.

That notion is as simple as it is misleading. But what it can do is help the decision maker avoid dead-end streets or would-be solutions that turn out to be cruel hoaxes. And with most social problems, there is little lead time to begin with. There is evidence of social scientists providing this service through their research if we quickly review the past decade. For example, in 1964 Martin Anderson showed that urban renewal reduces the housing supply rather than increasing it as had been assumed by housing experts for 25 years.

In 1965 Daniel P. Moynihan published a set of statistical correlations that showed that general economic conditions did not have a tight relationship to social structure as they had always had in the past. In 1966, James Coleman published his report, Equality of Educational Opportunity, which found, among other things, that there was little if any correlation between education inputs and educational results. Christopher Jencks, in 1973, confirmed this depressing hypothesis again. Shortly after the Model Cities program was announced in 1966, James Q. Wilson explained why this massive and costly program would fail. Two years later the White House understood this argument. And in 1969 the Westinghouse Learning Corporation evaluated the publicly acclaimed Head Start program and found it to have little impact. And of course there are other examples of social scientists applying their knowledge to social problems too numerous to list here. Perhaps it is understandable why the Social Science Research Council said in its 1968-69 report, "The difficulty we as a nation face in solving our problems is not will but knowledge. We want to eliminate poverty, crime, drug addiction and abuse; we want to improve education and strengthen family life, but we do not know how."

It is my belief that the future of the social scientist and his discipline need not be that of the role of a discredited charlatan when social problems are discussed in Washington and state governments. On the contrary, if steps are taken to draw the social scientist back into the arena of public life and arm him with the proper methodological skills, then he can become a powerful instrument in solving social problems. This is even more likely as politicians, planners, and key decision makers realize the need for relatively neutral data gathered in a systematic way on problems they are struggling with. They will have to make decisions on crucial issues whether or not they get any help from social scientists. It is in the interest of both that they do. If these changes occur, then the role of social science research in informing public policy will become even more important and necessary.

Thus, despite some setbacks, earned criticisms, and complex problems, the social scientist should not give up on the scientific game. In fact, each of these is a good reason to play at the game that much harder. Its value is obvious. Good, solid social science research can help improve decision making in the policy area. Good policy research has to consider or be made aware of all factual and normative variables that enter into a decision. A single isolated finding is not decisive. A decision to begin or stop an educational program is a whole community affair. More hard facts and opinions are needed by the policy maker than by anyone else. And this leads us full circle to where we began this chapter. Values and philosophy do play a bigger role in constructing a social science methodology than they did in conventional social science research of the past. Responsible social scientists should welcome the chance to enter the world of public policy because it is a necessary condition in the struggle for mankind and understanding.

REFERENCES

Blumer, Herbert. 1969. Symbolic Interactionism: Perspective and Method. Englewood Cliffs, N.J.: Prentice-Hall.

Coleman, James S. 1972. "Policy Research in the Social Sciences." Morristown, N.J.: General Learning Press.

Cowan, T. A. 1951. "A Postulate Set for Experimental Jurisprudence." Philosophy of Science 18.

Feyerabend, P. 1965. "Problems of Empiricism." In Beyond the Edge of Certainty, ed. Robert G. Colodny. Englewood Cliffs, N.J.: Prentice-Hall.

Forrester, J. W. 1961. Industrial Dynamics. Cambridge, Mass.: M.I.T. Press.

Kaplan, A. 1964. The Conduct of Inquiry. San Francisco: Chandler.

Kuhn, Thomas. 1962. The Structure of Scientific Revolutions. Chicago: University of Chicago Press.

Lekachman, Robert. 1976. "Social Science: The Public Disenchantment." The American Scholar, Summer.

Mayer, Martin. 1976. "Social Science: The Public Disenchantment." The American Scholar, Summer.

National Science Board, Special Commission on the Social Sciences. 1969. Knowledge into Action: Improving the Nation's Use of the Social Sciences. Washington, D.C.: Superintendent of Documents.

Nisbet, Robert. 1975. "Knowledge Dethroned." New York Times Magazine.

2
The General Systems Theory Paradigm

- If the complexities mentioned in Chapter 1 are to be adequately described, explained, and predicted, then a set of methodologies suited to such a task is needed. In fact, what is required is a new paradigm for guiding the assault on complexity. Such a paradigm amounts to a new type of scientific method.

It would appear that we have one on the near horizon in General Systems Theory (GST). I do believe that GST may be the most powerful methodology we have today for attacking complexity through scientific knowledge and using that knowledge to correct social ills.

As Kuhn (1970) has pointed out, a paradigm is much wider in scope than a theory but does function as an intellectual canopy for inquiry. In Chapter 1 I argued that the scientific methods of the natural sciences are not entirely adequate for coping with the life, behavioral, and social sciences. The application of such methods to these disciplines has not been as productive as in the physical sciences. The "scientific method" that was so useful in explaining physical systems must now be replaced with a new scientific method or "paradigm" to explain living systems. While physical and living systems share many common properties, new methods are needed to explain such living-system qualities as growth, change, adaptation, interaction, information processing, organization, decay, and death. This in turn means new ways of discovery, measurement, and hypothesis verification.

ORIGINS OF GENERAL SYSTEMS THEORY

General Systems Theory received its main impetus from Ludwig von Bertalanffy, a theoretical biologist (1950, 1952, 1967, 1968).

15

The late Von Bertanlanffy has contributed more than anyone else to the growth and development of GST and may be called "the father of GST." Early in his career Von Bertalanffy developed several basic concepts that described the organism as an open system. Later his biological theory of open systems was extended to psychology and ultimately into a general theory (General Systems Theory).

In the mid-1950s Von Bertalanffy was joined in the systems movement by such scholars as Kenneth Boulding, an economist (1956); J. G. Miller, a psychiatrist and psychologist (1955, 1965); W. R. Ashby, a bacteriologist (1958); and Anatol Rapoport, a mathematician (1956). Later contributions were made by such scholars as Walter Buckley, Magoroh Maruyama, Ervin Laszlo (1972), all of whom belong to a second generation of General Systems Theorists.

Certainly GST received invaluable contributions from C. E. Shannon in information theory, Norbert Wiener in cybernetics, and Ross Ashby also in cybernetics.

Thanks to these scholars Von Bertalanffy's earlier work has now spread to form a growing school of thought in many disciplines: in the behavioral sciences, Daniel Katz, Robert Kahn, and the late Kenneth Berrien; in the management and policy sciences, Ackoff, Churchman, Simon, Easton, Vickers, Lasswell, and Dror; in economics, Ken Boulding; in psychology, Allport, Piaget, Maslow, J. Bruner; in linguistics, Chomsky; in psychiatry, Menninger, Rizzo, Gray, and Watzlawick; in international relations, Schelling, Jandt, McClelland, and Quade; in political science, Deutsch; in philosophy, Laszlo; and in organizational theory, Weick.

GST is thus a young discipline still in its formative years. The Society for General Systems Research was organized only in 1954 and published its first Yearbook in 1956. Today there are three journals that publish articles on the General Systems Perspective as related to social and behavioral sciences: Behavioral Science, Human Relations, and the International Journal of General Systems. In addition there is the Journal of Mathematical Systems and publications of the Institute of Electrical and Electronics Engineers (IEEE), which publish articles on systems, cybernetics, feedback, and so on. Finally there is the British publication, International Journal of Systems Science.

Thus in approximately two decades GST has grown to the point where its claim as a new discipline is increasingly compelling. When combined with the effort that has been spent on its development and the pressure of societal problems, GST can no longer be ignored.

GOALS OF GENERAL SYSTEMS THEORY

A complex phenomenon is more than the simple sum of its parts or the properties of its parts. Such complex systems must also be explained in terms of the interactions or relations between the parts. It has taken man a long time to learn this lesson and it has been even more difficult for him to apply it. Modern science is still dominated by the ancient Greek concept of reduction, and mechanistic models still dominate.

GST is grounded in holistic methodology. We see today a shift in the social and behavioral sciences toward holism as a way of viewing the empirical world. This means one is forced to conceptualize in terms of wholes, forming connections to other wholes, heretofore thought to be isolated phenomena. It results in a rejection of the atomistic and mechanistic perspective. Thus the goal of GST is to view phenomena as wholes.

This goal is met by employing a number of different strategies. One of these is to try to bring order to chaos, pattern to randomness. The objective of the GST approach is not simply to describe nature, but to redefine nature as a piece of phenomenon that is an organized, interdependent set of elements. Thus chaotic randomness is redefined as organized complexity. This attempt to define wholes has resulted in an effort of finding analogies and isomorphisms between chemical, mechanical, and biological systems. Such conceptual links have been more of the anecdotal rather than experimentally derived data. These data do not weaken the GST concept but illustrate the difficulties of bringing living, complex systems into the confines of the laboratory.

Because of the complexity housed in a system, GST is as much a search for simplicity as it is for wholes. This might at first appear to be paradoxical, but in reality it is quite consistent. For example, if one is studying living biological systems—primates—one is struck by the similarity in behavioral traits between apes and man. Certainly the behaviors become more compex (such as speech) as one moves from a simple system to one of a higher order, but the point is that a common core of relationships appears in each system. Such relationships (speech) constitute a whole or become a system in themselves; the search for wholes has resulted in simplicity. Such an approach is justified on two levels. First, a search for simplicity is often a search for insights. Science, following its goal of parsimony, is clearly a search for simplicity, and thus GST is consistent with one of the canons of science. Second, as one reviews the social and biological world it would appear that the search for simplicity is an activity rooted in a survival mechanism. An environment that is simple and predictable is easier to survive or adapt to than a complex, random one. Certainly this has implications for man and other living systems trying to cope with social and ecological problems. General Systems Theory is concerned with rendering a complex environment simpler.

DEFINITION OF GENERAL SYSTEMS THEORY

Perhaps the time has come to offer a simple definition of GST: General Systems Theory is an attempt to postulate isomorphisms among fundamentally different phenomena. Behaviorally this means that the general systems theorist, in his research, searches for analogy-based principles or models that he can use to explain the behavior of phenomena. Viewed another way, Zadeh and Polak (1969) argue that while system theory is a discipline in its own right, it is also "a discipline which aims at providing a common abstract basis and unified conceptual framework for studying the behavior of various types and forms of systems."

From a phenomenological approach the general systems theorist attacks his problem under study through a methodological stance of holism that is guided by the emergent properties of the phenomenon itself, not by a priori hypotheses.

To help explicate this GST definition, Laszlo (1972) offers his "disciplinary matrix." GST may be considered a discipline because of the agreement among its practitioners that their problems and research take them across the narrowly defined traditional disciplinary boundaries. In looking at the general systems theorist one finds a man or woman who is well trained in a specific discipline but approaches the research problem from an epistemological awareness that he or she may have to pursue it in other areas. In short, GST is interdisciplinary.

"Matrix," according to Laszlo, refers to a set of assumptions in the form of principles or conceptual guidelines. Among these are holism as a methodology; the integration of scientific knowledge; and humanism as a task and responsibility of science.

Such a "disciplinary matrix" thus forms a philosophical base for GST and points it toward a quantitative-specific grounding. Such an orientation allows GST to translate the data it produces into practical terms for application to specific societal problems. Its ability to cross traditional discipline boundaries enables GST to produce these data.

ORGANIZATION OF GENERAL SYSTEMS THEORY

Boulding (1956) in his brilliant work, The Skeleton of Science, lays out two possible ways that GST might be organized. The first approach examines the empirical universe and selects certain general phenomena that are found in many different disciplines, and then attempts to build up general theoretical models relevant to these phenomena. The second approach attempts to arrange the empirical

fields in a hierarchy of complexity of organization based on their individual behavior, and then attempts to develop a level of abstraction
relevant to each.

For examples in the first approach, one might select constructs
like "information" or "communication." On one level of abstraction
one could look for communication phenomena (defined as the sending
and receiving of messages) in dyads, small groups, families, organizations, nations, and so on. Thus communication is a phenomenon
of almost universal significance for all disciplines in the social and
behavioral sciences. As Boulding notes, "Communication and information processes are found in a wide variety of empirical situations,
and are unquestionably essential in the development of organization,
both in the biological and the social world."

A second possible approach to GST is to arrange theoretical
systems or constructs in a hierarchy of complexity. This approach
may result in a system of systems.

Boulding's "skeleton" consists of nine levels of complexity.
The first level is that of a static structure known as frameworks. It
is the beginning of organized theoretical knowledge in any field corresponding to the geography and anatomy of the universe.

The second level is that of a simple dynamic system with prede-
termined, necessary motions similar to that of clockworks. Simple
equilibrium systems fit under this dynamic category, and most physical and chemical reactions and most social systems exhibit a tendency
to equilibrium.

On the third level is that of the control mechanism or cybernetic system, which Boulding calls the level of the thermostat. The
crucial difference between this system and the second level is the
transmission and interpretation of information. Here the system will
move to the maintenance of any given equilibrium, within limits. For
example, the thermostat will maintain any temperature at which it can
be set. The system at this level of complexity is concerned with the
difference between an "observed" or "recorded" value and its "ideal"
value—if the difference is not zero the system attempts to diminish
it; as with the thermostat turning on and off the furnace.

The fourth level is that of the "open system" or self-maintaining
structure. Since this is the level at which life begins it is called the
level of the cell.

The fifth level is called the genetic-societal level; it is represented by the plant. These systems are characterized by a division
of labor among cells to form a cell society with differentiated and
mutually dependent parts (seeds, roots, stems, leaves, and so on),
and "blueprinted" growth.

At the sixth level one has moved in complexity from the plant
world toward the animal kingdom. This "animal" level is typified by

increased mobility, teleological behavior, and self-awareness through the development of specialized information-receptors (eyes, ears, and so on) leading to a large increase in information processing ability. Also at this level the prediction of the behaviors of these systems becomes more difficult.

The seventh level is the "human" level with the individual (human being) considered a system. Particular characteristics include language and the ability to use symbols. It is the ability to use language as a symbolic activity rather than only as a sign, as with animals, that makes man human.

At the eighth level we find social organization. Here the unit of the system is not the human per se, but is best characterized as that of "role." One may define such social organizations (systems) as a set of roles tied together with channels of communication.

The ninth level is unknown. As Boulding wryly observes, "It will be a sad day for man when nobody is allowed to ask questions that do not have any answers!"

Boulding acknowledges that adequate theoretical models extend up to about the fourth level, but not much beyond. Empirical knowledge is deficient at all levels. Even at the first level, the problem of adequate description of complex phenomena is evident. Take a system like "education." The attempt to describe what constitutes the goals of an adequate learning environment is the subject of much debate among professional educators, much less parents.

One of the most valuable uses of Boulding's second approach is that each level incorporates all those below it. This suggests that insights can be obtained by applying low-level systems to high-level problems as, say, in the social world. Boulding argues that most of the theoretical ideas of the social sciences are still at level two, just rising to level three, although the subject matter clearly involves level seven. The history of psychology, for example, reflects its long inability to break free from a sterile stimulus-response model.

Boulding's second approach should make it clear to us that in dealing with societal problems we are attempting to cope with real-world systems that exceed our ability to conceptualize on these higher levels of complexity. This will often mean that our simpler systems (pet solutions) will let us down. Thus GST may point out how far we have to go in solving societal problems, but it provides a basis for hope in that it points out to some extent where we have to go.

THE NEED FOR GENERAL SYSTEMS THEORY

One does not have to be very bright, only to have lived a sufficient number of years, to recognize that societal problems are complex combinations of social, psychological, cultural, emotional, and economic factors with technological aspects. And everyone agrees that logical and effective approaches are needed to attack the problems if we are to get workable solutions. However, the issue is not the climate of heaven but how to get there.

Unfortunately there has been a parallel development in academic training and research leading to a huge "communications gap" between scientists. The present sociological state of science—emphasis on specialization—does not lead to holistic theory construction. This has resulted in a breakup of the body of knowledge, a resource desperately needed to solve complex problems in society. Hence, most social scientists do not converse with another because they have become too specialized, reflecting an earlier trend in medicine. There the general practitioner has almost ceased to exist. As Boulding (1956) observes, "One wonders sometimes if science will not grind to a stop in an assemblage of walled-in hermits, each mumbling to himself words in a private language that only he can understand." The more this trend toward specialization continues, the more likely communication between disciplines will decrease and the growth of knowledge will slow. On a more pragmatic basis, someone attempting to solve a complex societal problem will not know something he needs to know from another specialist. The lack of communication becomes a limiting factor on the chances of finding a solution.

In GST, concentration is on the analysis and design of the whole, differing from traditional science with its emphasis on the analysis and design of the components or the parts. The GST approach looks at the problem as a whole with all its facets evident. The end result is an attempt to develop a plan of analysis and action with specific combinations of specialists for solving the problem. In essence, GST functions as a communication methodology for unifying and integrating scientists from different disciplines. As a communication medium it makes possible the consideration of vast amounts of data and approaches necessary to solve complex, real-life problems. In a sense, there is perhaps a correlation between the growth of specialized disciplines and complex societal problems resulting in the need for an interdisciplinary discipline. Such a need has resulted in a GST that is concerned with the efficient employment of resources to the solution of problems.

It is important to point out here that while GST attempts to unify scientific disciplines, it does not seek to build a single "megatheory." Rather, its need is based on its aims: to discover similarities in different disciplines, and to develop a set of axiomatic statements that may perform the function of a gestalt in theory construction.

BASIC DEFINITIONS

System

A system is defined as a set of elements that are interdependent. The reader will note that this definition is general, but it permits any complex phenomenon to be included for purposes of analysis. Interdependent means that the elements of the system interact, and, more important, whatever affects one element will in some way affect all the other elements. The elements are the components or parts of the system.

Properties of Systems

Living and Nonliving Systems: Systems can be divided into two major classifications, living and nonliving. Living systems exhibit such biological functions as birth, growth, and death, while nonliving systems do not.

Abstract and Concrete Systems: An abstract system is one whose components are made up of concepts. Examples would be such elements as mathematical equations, words, rules, numbers, and so on. The sentence, "All men are mortal," could be viewed as an abstract system made up of the elements or components, words.

A concrete system is one that is physically real, composed of elements such as people, gases, rivers, trees, stars, computers, nations, tubes, wires, bones, genes, transistors, and so on. In short, a concrete system has a physical referent in the empirical world. All abstract systems are nonliving systems, but concrete systems can be living or nonliving.

Open and Closed Systems: An open system processes inputs from its environment. These inputs (stimuli), usually in the form of energy or information, are used by the open system to function. A closed system does not process inputs from its environment, but tends to function as a self-contained unit. In essence, a closed system has no environment. Any living system is an open system, because it must interact (exchange inputs) with its environment in order to survive. A digital wristwatch is a "closed" system and functions within itself as long as its battery is operational.

Another distinguishing characteristic between open and closed systems is growth. A living open system may process energy or information in order to change itself—in short, to grow. By "grow" one is not limited to an increase in physical size. An individual's brain (mind) may grow in terms of the ability to process information (think) without any change in physical weight. For example, a child's brain may grow in relation to an adult's as measured by an increased ability to use language.

However, a closed system does not have this capacity for growth. Such a system is restrained by its original configuration of components. It cannot grow into something else. In the earlier example of the wristwatch such a system can never grow into anything but a wristwatch, but a child, through the processing of energy and information, grows into an adult. The personality of a "healthy" individual may grow, but the personality of a paranoid schizophrenic is closed unless there is outside help.

The concept entropy, a measure of disorder or randomness borrowed from thermodynamics, is helpful in explication of open and closed systems. In an open system, entropy may increase, remain in a steady state, or decrease. In the short run, the second law of thermodynamics seems to be violated as living systems are able to avoid or reduce entropy. In the long run, the second law still holds as any living system will one day die with the system returning to entropy or randomness. But in the closed system, entropy never decreases. The matter-energy of the closed system is fixed at some maximum level and over time it will decrease. However slowly, the closed system relentlessly moves toward entropy or disorder, returning to its final state.

The distinction between open and closed systems is a crucial one for systemic thinking. GST, by making the distinction, freed life sciences from theoretical constructs and models based on classical physics and chemistry, which are of course closed systems. It is obvious that life-related phenomena interact with an environment and hence need a methodological approach that reflects an awareness of openness and all of its rich implications. Any analysis of open systems as closed systems, which ignores the environment and consequently such concepts as exchange, growth, interaction, and communication, will likely lead to erroneous conclusions. In psychiatry, early analysis began with a view of the mind as a diseased self-contained unit; clearly such a view was based on classical physics with its closed-system paradigm and naively neglected the idea that pathology may arise through interaction with others.

In fact, one can pick up the daily newspaper and find examples of well-meaning government officials and business managers persistently confusing an open system for a closed one with the predictable results.

Levels

One of the most powerful analytical tools in GST is the concept of levels. I might add that this notion is also one of great frustration in writing about GST, because of the difficulty in finding a beginning point. The fact that systems can be viewed as existing in a hierarchy suggests that there are levels of complexity in our systemic universe. Boulding's grouping of levels of systems toward increased complexity in the functions of components is one perspective. But here one is more interested in a simpler explanation of systemic hierarchy.

The concept of levels begins with the assumption that systems are embedded in other systems. For example, an atom may be viewed as a system. Such a system is embedded in a larger or more complex system, a molecule, or known in GST as a suprasystem. Looking in the other direction, inside the atom there is another system called an electron, or known as a subsystem. Thus the whole universe may be viewed as a hierarchy of systems. The management level of employees in an organization could be viewed as the suprasystem while the custodial staff would be viewed as a subsystem in such a hierarchy. Consequently, if one wanted to describe this organization in systemic terms, one would have the option of beginning the description at different levels—depending on the exact nature of the inquiry.

If one were conducting a content analysis of diplomatic messages the beginning point could be words, sentences, paragraphs, total transcripts, and so on. For instance, a system could be all declarative sentences with a suprasystem of paragraphs and a subsystem of words.

The flexibility of the researcher having the option to begin his analysis at different levels of a system accounts for much of the power of a systemic study. Such a viewpoint allows the investigator to see the interdependence between systems (as in air controllers and aircraft pilots) and environments (as in chemical waste and rivers). In short, living systems are no longer artificially isolated from one another; interaction and multicausality can be discovered.

Boundary

The boundary of a system is that area between it and another system. On a simple level, the walls of a room or one's skin constitute a boundary. On a more abstract level, the boundary of a computer is all of the functions it can perform. On still another level, the boundary of an organization is its marketplace.

Interface

Interface is a term used quite often in education circles. From a GST perspective, an interface is that area between the boundaries

of two or more systems. The Mississippi River represents an interface between two systems, St. Louis and New Orleans, as both cities
are connected by the great river.

State

The state of a system is defined as a particular arrangement
of components (elements) at a given point in time. Over time, a system's components may change in arrangement, but such a change
does not constitute a new system. Thus it is possible for a system to
have or occupy many different states. There is some minimum number of variables or components necessary for describing the state of
a system. To describe the financial state of an organization, various
accounting variables would have to be measured in order to define the
state of this system.

Inputs

A system's inputs are the energies absorbed by it or the information processed by it. Berrien (1968) asserts that inputs are of two
types: maintenance and signal. Maintenance inputs energize the system and enable it to function, while signal inputs provide the system
with information to be processed. Berrien provides a clear example
through the computer. In order to function, the computer must be
connected to some power source—this is a maintenance input. Once
energized, the computer follows a program and data to be processed
—these are signal inputs.

Such a distinction between inputs is extremely relevant because
living systems must process both types in order to survive. With a
living system, which by our earlier definition means that it must interact with its environment, it is not always easy to detect or distinguish
maintenance and signal inputs. For example, a work group in an organization that is deprived of communication will ultimately undergo
a decline in productivity if not disorganization. In this example it is
difficult to tell if the communicative input serves a maintenance or
signal function.

When considering an open system, two additional types of inputs
can be distinguished: controlled and uncontrolled. Controlled inputs
are ones the system can regulate, while uncontrolled cannot and are
usually unpredictable, such as events in nature (floods, droughts,
and so on). If the system cannot predict it, it is therefore uncontrollable.

Outputs

The outputs of a system are discharged into the suprasystem. Such outputs may be information, products, services, and energies. Such outputs may be useful to the suprasystem or unusable in the form of waste. It is possible to make a generalization here regarding outputs. If an output is not useful to some suprasystem somewhere in the environment, then the system will not survive. The old example of the buggywhip manufacturer comes to mind. In such a situation, the system must produce a different output that has demand or cease to exist.

The input-output behavior of a system raises an interesting point about GST that relates to the earlier discussion about system levels. A system may produce an output (a product, let's say),but this same bit of matter/energy becomes an input to the suprasystem. In short, our descriptive terms input and output depend, in the final analysis, on a particular perspective for their final classification. This aspect of GST is a rich but little-explored area of systemic research. It seems particularly so in the era of accountability when the worth of a social agency (welfare, for example) is evaluated. Or, consider the automobile as a system in Los Angeles. Is it worth retaining as a system of transportation? It provides inputs in the form of a means to get to work for millions of people. However, its output, pollution (smog), may destroy its suprasystem, automobile owners.

Berrien (1968) now raises the crucial argument. In the biological evolutionary process simple systems create complex systems, and in this life process a loop of input-output sequences was created that was self-supporting. In short, inputs and outputs assist the system in its quest for survival. In the course of evolution many systems have failed to survive. Perhaps an explanation of this can be found in the ratio of useful to useless inputs and outputs. If the ratio increased, the system tended to evolve toward increased complexity with a greater chance for survival. If the ratio decreased, useless outputs overcame useful ones, then the system and its suprasystem disintegrated. It would be interesting to apply this concept of living systems to such open systems as organizations, governments, nations, and so on.

The point here is that the suprasystem must select from the outputs produced by its subsystem. Appropriate selection is basic to the ultimate survival of the system. How it does this goes beyond the scope of this book to some degree, but today's social systems must define their inputs and outputs more precisely. This is underscored by the world's energy supply (fossil fuels), which we have learned painfully is finite. Also if an earlier point is recalled, that all systems are ultimately tied together, one realizes that the outputs of one system functionally determine what is produced by the next higher system. For instance, an infant lacking protein in his early diet may become mentally retarded. This tragic example reveals the interdependence of systems, and principles of GST apply to all levels, even though the inputs and outputs produced may be as different as amino acids and intelligence.

Feedback

Feedback is a central and perhaps the most important concept in GST. The interdependence between a system and its environment became apparent with the cybernetic concept of feedback. Cybernetics revealed that an output from a system was more than the mere transfer of energy; more important, it was information. This conceptual shift from energy to information meant that information about an effect, if "fed back" to the system (the effector), was a circular process, rather than linear. A circular view rather than the presupposed linear one meant that systems heretofore unexplained could now be analyzed. Such a model of causality is the proper one for interactional systems. The important functional implication of feedback is that a closed loop of action and reaction occurs. For instance, if system X produces output A that affects system Y then we have a deterministic linear system. But, if output A leads back to system X, the system is circular and functions differently. The conventional example of feedback is the thermostat and a furnace. If the temperature in the room drops below a preset temperature, the thermostat signals the furnace to turn on. At some point the temperature will rise to the prescribed setting, and the thermostat signals the furnace to turn off. This simple example illustrates the principle of feedback: The output of the system is measured and fed back to a control mechanism, which in turn regulates the inputs. Feedback thus allows a system to cope with disturbances and maintain the steady state of the system. Such disturbances need not be known beforehand, as in the case of an automatic pilot in an airplane keeping the aircraft level at a particular altitude. In both examples, part of the system's output as energy is reintroduced into the system as information about the output.

Negative and Positive Feedback

It is important to point out here that feedback may be either negative or positive. The reader should not jump to the lay usage of the terms to conclude that "negative" feedback is bad and "positive" feedback is good. The terms are used in the cybernetic sense.

Negative feedback characterizes a homeostatic or steady-state system and is therefore crucial in maintaining the stability of the system. With negative feedback, the feedback affects the system "negatively" in that any increase in the system's output is fed back, causing a regulatory action that tends to return the system to its previous steady state (equilibrium). In short, it can be said that negative feedback is deviation counteracting. This is illustrated in our furnace example where at some point the heat is turned on based on the discrepancy between actual and desired temperatures.

Certainly the concept of negative feedback can be applied to living systems with their behaviors of eating and sleeping. This can be applied to even more complex behaviors. Watzlawick (1967) offers this example. A family containing a schizophrenic member will react quickly and effectively to resist any attempt to change this individual since the stability of the family (system) depends on the continued organization or state of the family members. This resistance is a form of negative feedback returning the family system to its previous or steady state.

Positive feedback affects the system positively in that any change in the system's state causes more change, which results in the loss of stability or equilibrium. This "positive" move away from the norm may be seen in growth or a runaway process. In short, positive feedback is a deviation amplifying process. Examples in the empirical world are populations, communicable disease, rumor, cancer, and so on. Indeed, a large number of nonlinear systems, such as migration, can be described as positive feedback loops.

SUMMARY AND CONCLUSIONS

As a summary statement one can say that GST is a search for universals that can relate the specifics of different disciplines. This has resulted in a formal attempt to integrate similarities among the sciences, to increase communication among scientists, and to develop a theoretical base for axiomatic statements across all disciplines. GST attempts to counter the reductionistic approach of classical science with concepts of interaction, interdependence, communication, and organization.

A crucial concept to the development of GST has been holism, a philosophical perspective focusing attention on wholes. This means that the systems approach is one of conceptual problem solving, requiring an ability to perceive wholes, different levels, and interdependent relationships, rather than trying to reduce a problem to its parts. A system is not the sum of its parts. This is evident when the input-output discussion is recalled and it is realized that information cannot be added to or subtracted from a system without changing it.

All social systems may be described as complex, dynamic, open systems and therefore fit in the category of GST. Such a classification also means that one inherits societal problems. For instance, the current energy crisis must be viewed systemically. If one thinks of the energy shortage as simply a problem that can be solved by technology, then one has failed to understand an important lesson. Why did social scientists fail to point out that more economic growth requires more energy that in turn means more pollution? The present situation results from a failure to view the energy problem as a closed system with its inherent entropic nature. Recall that the entropy of a closed system continuously increases so that the order of the system steadily turns to disorder. Once a barrel of oil, lump of coal, or cubic foot of natural gas is burned, its chemical energy cannot be recovered. Substances can be recycled, but energy cannot.

Clearly what is needed is a holistic and flexible approach to problem solving, adaptable to different systems, at different levels, times, and environments. It is my conclusion that GST is such an approach.

REFERENCES

Ashby, W. R. 1958. "General Systems Theory as a New Discipline." General Systems Yearbook.

Berrien, F. K. 1968. General and Social Systems. New Brunswick, N.J.: Rutgers University Press.

Bertalanffy, L. von. 1950. "An Outline of General Systems Theory." British Journal of Philosophical Science 1.

_____. 1952. Problems of Life: An Evaluation of Modern Biological Thought. New York: Wiley.

_____. 1967. Robots, Men and Minds. New York: Braziller.

_____. 1968. General Systems Theory. New York: Braziller.

Boulding, K. 1956. "General Systems Theory—Skeleton of Science." Management Science 2.

Kuhn, Thomas. 1970. The Structure of Scientific Revolutions. Chicago: University of Chicago Press.

Laszlo, Ervin. 1972. The Relevance of General Systems Theory. New York: Braziller.

Miller, James G. 1955. "Toward a General Theory for the Behavioral Sciences." American Psychologist.

_____. 1965. "Living Systems: Basic Concepts." Behavioral Science.

Rapoport, Anatole. 1956. "The Diffusion Problem in Mass Behavior." General Systems Yearbook.

Watzlawick, P. 1967. Pragmatics of Human Communication. New York: Norton.

Zadeh, L. A. 1969. "The Concept of State in System Theory." In Views on General Systems Theory, ed. M. D. Mesarovic. New York: Wiley.

3

Graphics:
A Communication
Gestalt

It is reported that Soren Kierkegaard told the following parable:

It happened in a theatre that fire broke out in the wings.
Pajazzo came out to warn the audience. His message was
believed to be a joke and was met with applause; he reiter-
ated but was received with even louder cheers. Thus, I
imagine, the world will founder while all the witty heads
rejoice, convinced that it is a joke. (Schwarz 1973)

Communication is concerned with transmitting information so
that it is understood by the receiver. In Kierkegaard's parable it
was impossible for the clown's message to be understood despite the
seriousness of it.

In Chapter 1 the plea was made for a holistic methodology for
attacking social problems, and in Chapter 2 it was argued that General
Systems Theory could serve as a paradigm for this approach. In this
chapter an attempt will be made to underscore the crucial role of
communication in problem solving.

In modern society there are numerous equivalents to Kierkegaard's Pajazzo—well-meaning communicators who cannot make
themselves understood. Such communication breakdowns may be due
to many causes, but one of the more persistent reasons is perception.
The audience could not perceive that a clown should be taken seriously.
Thus we may conclude that the very medium (channel) used in a communication activity may establish perceptual limitations. To some
extent Marshall McLuhan is correct, the medium is the message. In
short, the way information is presented visually impacts on the receiver's perception of its clarity and credibility.

Coupled with this interesting interface between the communication medium (channel) and receiver's perception is another important link in the communication chain. Research by Broadbent (1965) and others would suggest a physiological limitation in addition to the psychological one mentioned above. It is found that the amount of information in a message increases up to a certain level and then remains constant as the input increases. As Broadbent argues, these findings suggest a communication capacity that is limited not by sensory factors alone, but by informational ones, which have in fact an upper limit for storing information. The often-heard expression, "I can't do two things at once," is an example of one's information input exceeding one's information storage capacity.

The idea of a limited information processing capacity and the message's channel affecting perception as key elements in the communication process has important implications for a methodology attempting to cope with societal problems.

As Broadbent states it, "We are measuring an inherent limit to human performance due to the capacity of the nervous system."

INFORMATION OVERLOAD

Information overload at the sensory level ultimately affects our perception of reality, and on the cognitive level it interferes with our ability to think. Since man is a homeostatic system he utilizes negative feedback loops to inform him about his relationship with his environment. To do this, an individual constantly processes information from his environment. All future behaviors thus depend on these information "readouts." As the environment becomes more novel and changing, an individual has to process more information in order to make intelligent decisions. This information requirement now raises the question of the channel capacity of a human being. Such a channel capacity may vary from individual to individual. Two conclusive statements can be made about this channel based on social science research: first, this human channel has a limited capacity; and second, information overload will have a negative effect on a person's performance. Miller (1964) asserts, "Glutting a person with more information than he can process may lead to disturbance." He suggests that information overload may be related to mental illness.

In society, the rate of change and complexity is rapidly increasing, yet we expect people to adapt to novel situations, confront and internalize complexity, and make rational decisions, all in shorter time periods. As citizens of a democracy they are expected to select various options toward solving a problem with very little lead time. The severe winter of 1977 and the systemic crisis it produced is a case in point. During that winter energy decisions had to be made ever faster as the problem worsened. By February there was no lead time left.

In short, people in today's society are forced to process information on complex problems at a much faster pace than at any other time in history. Such events are no doubt causing information overload in many of them, resulting in impacts that we can only speculate about.

SOCIETAL COMMUNICATION

As noted in Chapter 1, people are feeling overwhelmed by societal problems, but a number of them are questioning how we can cope with such complexity. Chapter 1 thus called for a methodology that could deal effectively with complex problems.

As any newspaper can demonstrate, complex societal problems are too difficult for even the "experts" to grasp. This has added significance for a democracy whose citizens must analyze, understand, and ultimately decide upon options when confronted with a problem. For these democratic processes to be successful, communication between large groups of people is necessary. And on another level, social scientists have to be able to communicate about complexity. Expertise and understanding have to be exchanged. Clearly, then, for this attack on complexity to take place communication is imperative.

THE NATURE OF COMMUNICATION

Miller (1965) expresses the view that information processing is one of two basic processes of living systems. If we extend this idea, communication may be defined as the process of information metabolism. Thus communication is as necessary to living systems as the processes involved in the metabolism of matter/energy. To an organism, then, communication is basic to all birth, growth, change, and survival processes.

For a human system there are two information exchanges with the environment: there are physical ones and there are those involving symbolic transactions.

The second exchange, symbolic interaction, is unique to the human organism. Only man has the ability to attach meaning through symbols to physical stimuli. Only a person can respond to the symbolic meaning of "honor." A dog or a horse, for example, could not. A man can have a referent for the word honor, whereas an animal cannot. It is the ability to symbolize that enables man to cope with complexity.

It is meaningful to divide human communication into three levels of activity. The first level, syntactics, is concerned with the accuracy with which symbols can be transmitted across a channel. This level is the primary concern of the information theorist. On the second level, semantics, the chief concern is with meaning. Do the transmitted symbols convey the desired meaning? On the third level, pragmatics, the focus is on the effects of the symbols. Thus all communicative activity may be analyzed and different questions raised under these three levels.

A few years ago communication theory was not a discipline in most universities, but today that has changed, and communication theory has emerged as a field of research. One of the reasons for this has been the exponential growth in the rate of technological change. This is obvious if one examines the dates of the major innovations in communication technology. The acceleration of change is evident if we examine the ages of communication media (De Sola Pool 1974):

Medium	Approximate Age in Years
Speech	500,000
Writing	4,000
Archives	2,000
Printing	500
Telegraph	140
Typewriter	110
Telephone	100
Radio	50
Television	25
Computer	25
Photocopying	20
Satellite	10

An examination of these dates would suggest that major communication media innovations will occur at least every decade. Thus we are in a period of massive communication change. How ironic that mediums that are supposed to facilitate understanding now are contributing to the information overload mentioned earlier in this chapter.

It is difficult to predict all of the pragmatic (level three) effects of such innovations, but there is ample social science research evidence to suggest a causal relationship between the growth of mass media and the acceleration of change. This idea was discussed some years ago by the late Harold A. Innis. Innis (1951) argued that new communication technologies alter societies in rather profound ways. He suggested that knowledge or an oligopoly of knowledge is built up to the point that equilibrium is disturbed. In short, each new communication innovation (technology) forces a realignment in the monopoly of knowledge. For example, the Greeks invented the alphabet and made it into a flexible instrument tailored to the demands of a flexible oral tradition by the creation of words, and a new learned ruling elite emerged. Thus sudden extensions of communication produce cultural disturbances.

If a medium of communication has profound effects on the dissemination of knowledge over space and time, it would seem important to recognize the communication bias of the period in which we live and work. It would also seem logical to try to develop communication technologies that would have predictable effects. It would seem that we could take the offensive in dealing with societal problems by employing a communication medium that would have a positive effect on such difficulties.

As pointed out in Chapter 1, a tremendous step toward coping with social ills would be the development of a method for conceptualizing about them. In other words, why not let a communication medium lead the assault on complexity? Why not a communication medium (or innovation) that would allow us to conceptualize better?

Earlier it was argued that to cope with complex societal problems a new methodology for examining such problems is needed. One was offered in a holistic perspective or methodology. Then the argument was developed for a new paradigm and it was suggested that this was available in General Systems Theory. Now what is needed is a method to energize these two powerful concepts. It is suggested here that such a catalyst is found in a new communication medium. In short, a new communication language is needed to deal with today's complexity. This chapter will attempt to explore such a language.

THE MEANING OF MEANING

Before such a language can be discussed it is necessary to explore in more detail the subjective nature of communication. While a physical science attempts to deal with facts, measurement, and prediction, a human science (actually, all social sciences) must deal with meaning(s). This means that a person communicating can be both the object and subject of his communication or message. We are concerned not only with his communicative behavior but also the meaning of that behavior. Now we see that human communication has a relational aspect to it as well as a mere physical one (that is, the actual words used).

Blumer (1969) says, "The nature of an object consists of the meaning that it has for the person for whom it is an object." According to Blumer, meaning is a social product created by humans as they interact or communicate. Meanings are not in words, but in people. For example, Whitehead (1958) illustrates that information is processed either directly (as one is slapped on the face) or through symbolic interpretation (as when one understands the meaning of a slap on the face).

To cope with complexity thus becomes more difficult than we had imagined since we must also allow for subjective meanings. This means that we may have trouble even agreeing on the nature or parameters of a problem. But a beginning point would be to make sure that all the discussants are at least discussing the same issues. How often have you been engaged in a discussion about a complex problem when someone begins to talk about a problem or issue that has nothing to do with the one at hand? It would appear the more complex the issue the more likely this is to happen. The solution is obvious. We must find a way to communicate clearly, concisely, and with increased fidelity.

INFORMATION THEORY

Since the publication of Wiener's Cybernetics (1948) there has been much intellectual excitement about the application of information theory constructs to human perception and decision making.

Information theory was originally concerned with communication problems at level one, syntactics. It was largely one concerned with mechanistic problems, that is, how to transmit a signal across a channel with a given amount of noise (unwanted disturbance). The basic question is, "How does a sender get his message across a channel, given some inherent level of noise, so that a receiver can understand it?"

A simple question, but one not easily answered because of the complicated nature of "information." It is assumed that the sender begins with freedom of choice as to what symbols he will encode or send. The receiver has the problem of reconstructing the message from the symbols he receives. Darnell (1971) makes the interesting observation that the receiver's uncertainty about the transmitted message is precisely equal to the source's freedom of choice in constructing the message.

Consequently, information comes to be a mathematical concept grounded in such constructs as freedom of choice, uncertainty, and entropy. The information of a given system is best described as freedom of choice or alternatives available to it. Generally speaking, the more alternatives means the more information available. For instance, there is more information contained in a typewriter with 42 keys than a machine containing only 26 keys. Or the statement, "Jon has narrowed his college choices to four—Stanford, Harvard, Princeton, and Yale—all with a 25 percent probability," contains more information than "Jon has decided to go to Stanford."

Thanks to Shannon (1949) we have a mathematical equation that measures information:

$$H = -\sum p_i \log p_i$$

The base-two logarithm in the equation defines the unit of information as the bit, which is the amount of information involved in a choice between two equally probable alternatives. Thus the value of the equation is unity (one) when exactly two alternatives are considered with each having the probability of .5 and the $\log_2$ is entered. If I ask you if you want to go to a movie, and you answer either "yes" or "no," then your answer produces about one bit of information.

Given this base, it would seem to be a small cognitive leap to try to extend information theory (level one, syntactics) to the second level, semantics. This means that one must deal with meaning. Most communication research studies have been source biased. Perhaps it would be useful to recall information as defined as freedom of choice or alternatives, and then to extend this construct to the "response" of the receiver. In other words, the receiver also has freedom of choice through the many "meanings" he might attach to the received message. In essence, such an interpretation means we are dealing with the problem noted earlier in the chapter: the difficulty of getting people to agree on the "meaning" of a complex problem. What needs to be done in information theory terms is to reduce the "uncertainty" in a message to zero. We want to eliminate any "alternative" interpretation as to the nature of the problem under discussion. The success of our attack on complexity may be determined by the amount of uncertainty we can remove when discussing the problem.

INFORMATION AND STRUCTURE

The information theory developed by Shannon was based on a theory of randomness of independent events. Thus a system built on random independent events would likely be more simple than complex and display a highly probable state of homogeneity. Maruyama provides a clear and brilliant example (1973). If the sand on the beach is blown in all directions by a more or less random wind, the surface of the beach is fairly homogeneous. It is highly improbable that the winds would build a complex sand castle. According to Maruyama, then, the general rule of the universe is homogenization, if one accepts the assumptions of 1949 information theory.

But there are problems with such an assumption of homogeneity, because we know evolutionary processes often lead to more complex organisms. Biologists have observed this for a long time, but in 1960 a Russian mathematician, Stanislaw Ulam, was able to demonstrate this mathematically. Ulam (1962) was able to show that complex patterns can be generated by simple rules of interaction. Interestingly, it takes more information to describe the resulting patterns than the rules that produced them. Perhaps of even more interest, it is often impossible to determine the generating rules from the final patterns, suggesting once again that the whole is greater than the sum of its parts.

Now it is here that Maruyama (1973) offers a revolutionary insight: We may have been misguided by the classical model of homogeneity to assume that what survives is the strongest, but actually what may be happening in evolution is the process of heterogenization, and what survives is not the strongest but what is the most symbiotic. In other words, the organism that is most likely to survive is the one that can associate or live with a dissimilar organism.

This leads to confirmation of the expectation that the model of the universe is one of mutual causal relations reflecting symbiotic behavior. For example, in my tropical fish aquarium I have a number of living plants that produce oxygen. The fish breathe the oxygen and give off carbon dioxide, and the plants convert this carbon dioxide into oxygen. In this system, then, life processes are maintained by the interdependence of different living systems. What a difference heterogeneity makes. It seems logical to conclude that society as a living system is always evolving toward increased complexity or heterogeneity.

Now we get to the importance of communication. If man, as the only symbol-using animal, is evolving toward increased heterogeneity, he must find a way to be symbiotic—to interact with other ecological and human systems. A way must be found to combine various needs, wants, and desires into some type of symbiotic network. Members of a society must improve their symbiotic behavior through their most powerful skill—the ability to communicate.

It is no mere coincidence that the crisis in society occurs at the same time as our crisis in communication. Likewise, it is no accident that social science research has not explored the relationship between communication and symbiotic processes. To do this type of research will require a radical departure from our previous assumptions, methods, and models. In Kuhn's famous phrase, we need a "scientific revolution."

There is precedent for this in societal behavior. Lawson (1975) argues, "There has appeared an entirely new code or language system that functions in the social development and social integration of

individuals. Human society seems to be a culmination of an evolutionary process that has produced successive levels of integration, by
the creation of new levels of intercommunication." It is the task now
to speculate on what this new code or language system might be.

MANY-BODY PROBLEM

As noted earlier, societal problems are complex ones compounded by the difficulty of treating such complexity systematically.
Moynihan (1972) comments on this difficulty:

> Anthropologists tell of a people so indifferent to complexity
> that the whole of their numerical system consists of the
> terms "one," "two," and "many." And yet how close to
> our own reality they are. It is hard enough to keep two
> things in mind; more than that becomes immensely diffi-
> cult. A while back, one of Harvard's great chemists was
> discoursing on what he called the "many-body problem,"
> a condition in which the number of variables interacting
> with one another in any given situation makes that situa-
> tion extraordinarily complicated and difficult to fathom.
> I asked in what range of numbers this many-body problem
> begins. A somewhat suspicious glance was returned.
> Did I really not know? Apparently not. "Three," he re-
> plied.

Moynihan goes on to note:

> This is an aspect of our reality. It becomes significant
> with the onset of what James C. Coleman terms an "infor-
> mation-rich society." Such a society is not necessarily
> better able to handle itself. For people, as for rats, too
> much contradictory information is disorienting, and there
> follows the impulse to get back to simple things. Social
> science needs a strategy for dealing with this condition.
> The various disciplines wish to become ever more com-
> plex in order, interalia, to provide "more reliable guides
> to public policy." But as complexities compound them-
> selves, the public is likely to ask for ever more simpli-
> city.

Thus it seems the social scientist is charged with discovering
the necessary elements of a methodology for coping with complexity.

COUNTERINTUITIVE BEHAVIOR

Moynihan points out the almost impossible task of keeping complex issues in our head. Forrester (1971) notes the same difficulty when trying to think about social systems. We try to think about them, Forrester says, by carrying mental images in our head. Such an image of the world becomes a model for organizing and directing behavior. The problem, according to Forrester, is that the mental model is fuzzy and incomplete. It is this way because one cannot carry a government or a city or a social problem like energy in his head. What the individual does carry are bits and pieces that he uses to represent the real system. In addition, in a communicative interaction situation, such as a heated discussion, the model may vary. As more people enter the discussion, each with his own subjective model, different interpretations of the subject arise. And often the basic assumptions the participants bring to the discussion are never revealed. It is not surprising that understanding takes so long,if it ever occurs. But the most important difficulty between the mental model and the real system appears in the dynamic consequences when the assumptions within the model interact with one another. The many-body problem again. The human mind, operating on its mental model, is not capable of sensing all the interdependencies of the elements in the real system. The failure of the human mind via its mental model is clearly evident when "well-reasoned" solutions to social problems fail.

Forrester has demonstrated in his research in computer simulation that often our intuitive models fail to predict the behavior of real-world systems. This occurs because socioeconomic-environmental systems are multiloop, nonlinear feedback systems whose structures do not resemble the simplistic models we carry in our heads. Winthrop (1972) calls for efforts in planning and policy making that will accurately capture the structures of complex systems.

It would seem to me that structural predictions should become one of the chief methodological concerns of social and behavioral scientists. We must begin to develop ways for describing and measuring the parameters of a social problem. If we are unable to do this, then all of our mental models will have an inherent source of error resulting in erroneous predictions. Forrester cites pitfalls that may likely result from error inherent in mental models:

Policies designed to correct problems in one social system may produce or worsen another set of problems in that same system.
A short-term policy often fails to see long-term consequences that may appear at a later date.
One may solve the problems of a subsystem only to hinder or undermine the goals of the suprasystem.

Real-world examples of such dangerous results are abundant. A "fast" lane requiring three or more people in a car is created only to have the other lanes become more crowded as a result of the loss of that lane. A business with falling profits raises the price of its products only to have a drop in demand with the result that profits are now at a lower level. A public utility company is allowed to burn "dirty" coal in place of natural gas in order to save money only to spew more pollution into the atmosphere. And certainly the reader can think of personal experiences in which the solution becomes the problem.

PARADIGMS AND COMMUNICATION

Maruyama (1974) argues that the communication difficulty between problem solvers is not that the parties use different vocabularies to talk about the same thing, but rather that they use different structures of reasoning. In the resulting interaction, each party attributes the breakdown in communication to the other person's closed mind, ignorance, lack of intelligence, or insincerity.

Any thinking individual is aware that there are different logics of "proof." Methods of proof may include historical evidence, critical acclaim, or empirical data all leading to different structures of reasoning. Thus we may get ourselves into communication cul-de-sacs because we are unable to follow the other person's reasoning. The point here is not to argue as scientists versus humanists, but to observe the reality that there are different structures of reasoning between individuals, professions, and cultures. To solve immense complex societal problems, we must find a way of communicating despite different thought processes.

COMMUNICATING ABOUT COMPLEXITY

The reader will recall the earlier definition that a system is a set of elements that are interdependent. Using this systemic definition, we can search for a method to overcome the communication snag caused by different structures of reasoning. What are the necessary "elements" for coping with complexity? It would seem to me that some of these elements would need to be methodological tools that are concerned with defining the structure of complex problems. These would become necessary, but not sufficient, conditions for solving complex problems.

A solution may be found if it is remembered that complex issues have both structure and content. Now if a way can be found to commu-

nicate about the structure, the content can be worried about later.
Structure must be dealt with first.

It has been my observation in problem solving that often the communication bottleneck is a failure of the interested parties to see the
structure of the issue. Much of this failure is due to the immense
complexity or many-body nature of real systems. So communication
strategy must become that of finding a way of making structure physically real—as on paper or chalkboard—so that structure is stored
and the mind is free to think about content.

Gerard (1968) has postulated three basic elements of systems:
structure, function, and evolution. The structure of a system is the
pattern of matter in space and is concerned with the relationships
among the components. If a system is structured it possesses order.
Consequently, a system's function is its pattern of relationships
among components. Thus structure is concerned with order and function with complexity.

An understanding of structure and order for a communication
system is the beginning point for an inquiry into complexity. Miller
(1965) has suggested that scientific research needs to discover structure before the dynamics of interaction can be explored.

This leads us to an interesting observation. The methodologies
we employ for problem solving should be evaluated for their communicative ability more than their scientific rigor. This does not mean
they are not scientific. On the contrary, it is assumed they would be.
But the emphasis must be on their communication qualities if we are
to create structure—and thereby overcome complexity. The parties
to the problem-solving exercise must be able to communicate. The
structure of the problem must be identified for everyone.

The basic elements of communication methodologies should be
common to all problem-solving communication systems. Such elements
would include symbols (words), rules (mathematics), and graphics.
The first two are easily recognized as common communication elements, but the last, graphics, has not been fully developed as a communication tool. Such an element is crucial to problem solving because it offers the most promise for creating structure. If the mind
can be freed of structure through graphics, then the intellect can focus on the content and interaction aspects of the problem.

A COMMUNICATION GESTALT

Society's problems have at their core a communication problem.
Despite the evolution in communication techniques, the various media
have remained essentially linear. Such a classical approach—with
its left-to-right sequence, single cause-and-effect explanations and

prescriptions, and large amounts of technical jargon—fails to build structure. More important, such a medium cannot communicate gestalt. If society is to be made manageable, gestalt communication languages must be discovered and utilized. If a holistic perspective, as called for in Chapter 1, is to be developed, then a communication language or medium that conveys wholes must be implemented. A dialogue must be established between those who have some knowledge or insights to the problem at hand. But there is a basis for hope if communication can jump from a linear to a gestalt mode.

Here we are arguing that graphics is a gestalt communication mode. It provides an overall picture of the problem in such a way that the reader or viewer can grasp the wholeness of it. It provides structure and wholeness at once. It is offered as a new communication language because of its propensity for conveying holistic perspectives. If I may offer a subjective observation, graphics, as a new communication mode, appears to be "right-brained." Psychological research is beginning to offer evidence that the left side of the brain deals with analytical, sequential logical functions, but the right side copes with wholes or gestalt-like problems. The two sides use different languages with the right side expressing itself with imagery and forms. In order to communicate with the right side, a language must be used that is holistic. Or put another way, if we want to see the forest rather than the trees we must use right-brain language.

The value of graphics as a medium for communicating gestalt is reflected in catastrophe theory. Based largely on the work of Rene Thom, professor of mathematics, catastrophe theory describes phenomena (not always disasters) that switch abruptly from one form of behavior to a radically different one. Catastrophe theory belongs to the branch of mathematics known as topology, a field (like geometry) that deals with phenomena not only numerically but also visually. Through catastrophe theory, discontinuous events like earthquakes, stock market crashes, or cell divisions can be represented by certain geometrical shapes. Topologists use increasingly complex pictures in which catastrophes are represented by "peaks," "slopes," "troughs," "cusps," and "pleats" in surfaces. As Lynn Arthur Steen, a mathematician, explains, "When the mind must work only with numbers, it works linearly, on one track, but if a particular problem can be transformed into a picture, then the mind grasps the problem as a whole and can think creatively about solutions."

Such support and understanding from complex mathematics offers more evidence that difficult social problems are best attacked by conveying their gestalts. It might be important to pause here and define gestalt. "Gestalt" is a German word meaning the way a physical entity, experience, or phenomenon has been made or put together, referring to the pattern or shape of it. Extending the gestalt idea, its chief principle emerges that the whole is greater than the sum of its parts. The converse being that an analysis of a phenomenon's parts will not explain the whole. The latter statement is now supported by the mathematician Ulam's work noted earlier in this chapter.

In order to deal with complexity, new methodologies are needed. Through graphics it is possible to portray a gestalt-like statement about a complex problem identifying its structure, elements, and dynamic interaction. The generation of successful solutions to societal problems requires effective communication. What is needed the most are methodologies that are scientifically rigorous and at the same time effective tools of communication. Communication between social and behavioral scientists must be broadened to include more than the verbal exchange of messages, and now must include graphics. Since we earlier defined societal problems as real systems having elements and relationships between them, so must our methodologies contain these constructs. If we are concerned with a problem like welfare reform, we must through our methodology identify the crucial welfare elements and the interactions that occur between them. Hence, we arrive at our earlier position: The burden of communicating about a "many-body" problem falls on the graphic mode.

If we work backward for a moment and recall that in General Systems Theory all systems are hierarchically organized, then it seems logical to extend the concept of hierarchies to complexity. Simon (1969) points out the frequency with which complexity takes the form of hierarchy. Research in studying complexity suggests that the best method of attack is to reduce the complexity to elements and relations. Graphic communication is particularly suited for doing this. Through its emphasis on structure, it identifies the elements of the problem and reveals relationships between them. From such a base the problem solvers are then in a position to deal with the unique content of the phenomenon.

While a graphic communication may become exceedingly complex, all graphs begin with elements and relationships. A common starting point for graphic communication media is the bipartite graph (Friedman 1969). It is called a bipartite graph because the "bi" represents the two basic graph symbols. The circle refers to an element and the square a relationship. For example, the statement, "There is a relationship between poverty, population, and crime," can be expressed in a bipartite graph. See Figure 3.1.

The reader will note that the graph does not state the nature of the relationship, only that one exists. A relationship might be direct (positive) or inverse (negative). If there is a direct causal relationship from one element to another, changes will occur in the same direction. If there is an increase in one element, there will be an increase in the other element; and if there is a decrease in one element, there will be a decrease in the other. So with a direct causal relationship there can be either increases or decreases. With an in-

FIGURE 3.1
A Bipartite Graph

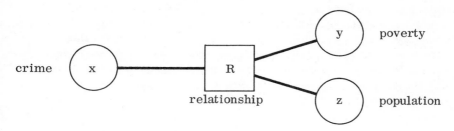

Source: Compiled by the author.

verse, or negative, causal relationship one element changes in one direction and another element changes in the opposite direction. For example, disease and population growth usually reflect an inverse relationship in poor nations. Any real system is composed of many causal relationships, some direct and some inverse, and to understand the system we must identify all the causal relationships. If we are able to do this, we can determine the consequences of the entire pattern of relationships.

For one conducting social science research or advising policy issues there are many real-world systems composed of elements with unspecified relationships. Often one is aware that there is a relationship between certain known elements, but one is unable to say whether the relationship is direct or inverse. However, what the graphic communication medium does is to establish that a relationship exists without cluttering the thinking with speculations about the nature of it. If it can be agreed that a relationship exists, at a later date data can be collected to explain the exact nature of it. As social scientists we then start with a basis of agreement: that a relationship exists. The graph provides fundamental structure for a many-body problem, and we have a beginning point for investigating the nature of specific relationships.

As a communication tool the bipartite graph is a powerful instrument. It is context free. That is, any problem can be expressed using its basic symbols of elements and relationships. In addition, it is very parsimonious, eliminating the redundancy found in verbal or written statements. By this it enables one to focus on the essentials of the problem, facilitating understanding and insight. Finally, the size of the graph does not increase as quickly as a corresponding written explanation despite the number of elements and relationships involved. This means the problem–solver can identify crucial elements and relationships and build upon them later.

This is illustrated in Figure 3.2. Suppose that we want to explore the real–world system of television, children, and violent behavior. We can begin to get a perspective on this complex issue if we utilize a graphic communication medium. We can do this by letting numbers refer to the system's elements and letters represent the relations between them. The structure of the problem is captured by the graph.

FIGURE 3.2
An Extended Bipartite Graph

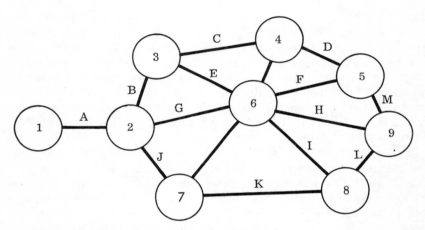

Source: Compiled by the author.

Thus 9 elements and 13 relationships have been identified. The graph provides a gestalt by linking all the elements and their relationships into a systemic whole. The heuristic value of such a graph is evident with the emergence of the elements and their interdependent nature. It is important to recall that earlier in the chapter Forrester (1971) noted that the counterintuitive nature of social systems was due to the failure of the researcher or policy maker to capture the structure of the system and its subsequent dynamics. Graphic communication is an attempt to deal with this problem.

Graphic communication may be used to cope with an existing problem, or it may be used in a hypothetical one. It is reported that Watson and Crick in their research on the DNA molecule had trouble conceptualizing about its molecular structure. They solved the problem by getting the familiar Tinker Toy game and from it constructed a laige wooden model that they thought represented the DNA molecular structure. Thus graphic communication media can be used for hypothesis testing and theory construction.

The reader may note the similarity between Figure 3.2 and a flow chart. This is inherent because of the great ability of a flow chart to convey gestalt or holistic imagery. While a flow chart is linear or sequential, to some extent the user of such an instrument can select alternate paths for meeting his objectives as in program evaluation review technique (PERT) or critical path method (CPM). The main value of all flow charts is that through their creation of structure they convey the wholeness of the system. It may be helpful to think of the function of a flow chart as that of a map. A map is not read in a linear fashion, but rather the map is used for problem solving—how do I get from point A to point B. Maps take essential elements like towns and link them through highways and roads and the reader has the choice of different routes. In short, he may begin at any point, depending on where he wants to go. In contrast to linear prose a map has no beginning or end. Consequently, a map conveys a gestalt. Like a map the purpose of a graphic flow chart is to convey the imagery of a whole system. Since the structure of the problem is stored on paper, one's mind is free to follow the logic or chain of events that is expected to occur.

Other chapters in this book will deal with particular methodologies similar to flow charts in that they attempt to convey a gestalt or wholeness perspective, and they are concerned with identifying the problem's structure, elements, and relationships. These will include chapters on objectives trees (Chapter 6), DELTA charts (Chapter 7), Delphi technique (Chapter 8), cross-impact analysis (Chapter 9), and scenario construction (Chapter 10).

THE LANGUAGE OF THE FUTURE

In the era of future shock, there is an urgent need for a new language of problem solving. Such a language would have as its syntax a highly communicative set of methodologies or tools that allow one to deal with new and emerging problems, having no precedent, in a way that promotes understanding.

It is argued that such a language can be a powerful tool for coping and explaining complex issues like societal problems. Such a language is not a panacea for solving very real-world problems like crime, poverty, energy, and so on. But it is most useful as a heuristic device because it provides perspectives not found in traditional languages. To extend an analogy: Old-world languages function like the reading of a long, detailed Victorian novel, whereas the new language, based on graphics, functions like a film based on the novel. Certainly much detail is left out, but the movie communicates a whole or gestalt perspective that would be hopelessly lost in the details of the novel. A picture is worth a thousand words.

The central thesis of this chapter has been that a new language for coping with complexity must be developed. Given the enormity and many-body nature of real-world problems, one's mental capacity for storing all the necessary information breaks under the strain. Because we have little lead time for problem solving, another method of conveying information is imperative. Because man must now deal with many futures, he must find a way to comprehend the future. Our old languages do not provide us with a satisfactory way of doing this because they cannot communicate the gestalt now needed.

The language of the future will take many forms, but the core will be based on graphics as outlined in this chapter. It is a communication medium not well understood since it is still in its infancy. But in research and development (R&D) organizations there are some encouraging results from its usage. Although a hybrid form of communication, it represents the first attempt to develop a language of the future. It is an attempt to move communication from a linear origin to a gestalt mode. Because of the complexity of our modern problems, the failure of most solutions to solve them, and the rapidity of their occurrence, there is a sense of urgency to developing this new language form. There are tremendous obstacles to be overcome before we have a highly effective gestalt communication medium, but there are some hopeful signs about its development, and since hope is a sentiment I cherich I am confident it is an idea whose time has come.

REFERENCES

Blumer, H. 1969. Symbolic Interactionism. Englewood Cliffs, N.J.: Prentice-Hall.

Broadbent, D. E. 1965. "Applications of Information Theory and Decision Theory to Human Perception and Reaction." In Cybernetics of the Nervous System, ed. N. Wiener and J. P. Schade. Amsterdam: Elsevier.

Darnell, D. 1971. "Information Theory." In Communication: Concepts and Processes, ed. J. A. DeVito. Englewood Cliffs, N.J.: Prentice-Hall.

De Sola Pool, Ithiel. 1974. "The Rise of Communications Policy Research." Journal of Communication 24, no. 2 (Spring).

Forrester, Jay W. 1971. "Counterintuitive Behavior of Social Systems." Technology Review, January.

Friedman, G. J., and C. T. Leondes. 1969. "Constraint Theory." IEEE G-SSC Transactions 5, nos. 1, 2, and 3.

Gerard, R. W. 1968. "Units and Concepts of Biology." In Modern Systems Research for the Behavioral Scientist, ed. W. Buckley. Chicago: Aldine.

Innis, Harold A. 1951. The Bias of Communication. Toronto: University of Toronto Press.

Lawson, Chester A. 1975. "Biological Organization." In General Systems Theory and Human Communication, ed. B. Ruben and J. Kim. Rochelle Park, N.J.: Hayden.

Maruyama, Magoroh. 1973. "A New Logical Model for Futures Research." Futures, October.

_____. 1974. "Paradigms and Communication." Technological Forecasting and Social Change 6.

Miller, James G. 1964. Disorders of Communication, vol. 42. Research Publications Association for Research in Nervous and Mental Disease.

_____. 1965. "Living Systems." Behavioral Science 10.

Moynihan, Daniel P. 1972. "The Schism in Black America." The Public Interest, Spring.

Schwarz, S. 1973. "Aspects of Visual Communication and the Future." Technological Forecasting and Social Change 4.

Shannon, C. E., and W. Weaver. 1949. The Mathematical Theory of Communication. Urbana: University of Illinois Press.

Simon, H. A. 1969. The Sciences of the Artificial. Cambridge, Mass.: M.I.T. Press.

Ulam, Stanislaw. 1962. "On Some Mathematical Problems Connected with Patterns of Growth Figures." Proceedings of Symposium on Applied Mathematics 14.

Whitehead, Alfred North. 1958. Symbolism. New York: Macmillan.

Wiener, Norbert. 1948. Cybernetics. New York: Wiley.

Winthrop, Henry. 1972. "Social Systems and Social Complexity in Relation to Interdisciplinary Policy Making and Planning." Policy Sciences 3.

4
Policy Sciences

Suppose you own a pond on which a water lily is growing. The lily plant doubles in size each day. If the lily were allowed to grow unchecked, it would completely cover the pond in 30 days, choking off the other forms of life in the water. For a long time the lily plant seems small, and so you decide not to worry about cutting it back until it covers half the pond. On what day will that be? On the 29th day, of course. You have one day to save your pond.

This little story is an attempt to illustrate the necessity of sound policy making for coping with today's societal problems and to show how catastrophe can occur without it.

By way of metaphor this chapter, in fact the entire book, is concerned with saving the pond. My optimism comes from the belief that our problems, as complex as they are, like the pond, can be saved if reason and hard work are applied. Though the problems are novel, we do have fairly new methodologies for attacking them. This chapter on policy sciences represents the main assault with the following chapters acting as waves of attack.

Policy sciences is something of a supradiscipline—to use General Systems Theory language—that is concerned with improving policy making. These improvements will come from social and behavioral science knowledge, structured rationality, and new uses of the scientific method.

This chapter will attempt to offer a workable alternative to the thesis of the first three chapters, namely, that traditional social science methodology is inadequate to solve today's societal problems. Clearly, this means that radical or new scientific paradigms, methodologies, and purposes are required. Policy sciences as a movement or field does attempt this and in so doing tries to tell policy makers how to make better decisions.

The relation between the social sciences and policy-making efforts toward the solution of societal problems has become more apparent in recent years. On occasion, the two "worlds" do interact and often with mixed results. The belief that this interaction could be made more beneficial to both social scientists and policy makers is why this book was written.

Although the original conception of policy sciences was laid out by Lerner and Lasswell (1951) about 25 years ago, the field has begun to emerge only in the last ten years. There are several key reasons why the field has grown so rapidly in recent years. First, there is the relentless push of today's problems. Like a fault zone running through the 1960s, the stress and strain of poverty, energy, and ecology have produced a crack in the crust of the 1970s that cannot be ignored. Second, there is considerable dissatisfaction of clients and governmental policy makers with social scientists and the application of their knowledge to contemporary issues. Fortunately, the idea still exists among some of those in power that social science knowledge should and could be utilized. And third, there are some social scientists who want to use their training and expertise to produce solutions to concrete real-world problems.

POLICY SCIENCES AND HAROLD LASSWELL

The intellectual father of policy sciences is Harold Lasswell. In 1951 he and Daniel Lerner edited The Policy Sciences with Lasswell writing an introductory essay that spelled out the aims of the field. Unfortunately, the book was largely unnoticed by social scientists, but in 1971 Lasswell published his A Pre-View of Policy Sciences with much more impact. Apparently certain necessary events have occurred for the book to exert the influence it deserves. It is difficult to discuss any policy sciences concept that is not touched by Lasswell's 1971 edition.

In A Pre-View Lasswell offers a working definition of policy sciences: "The policy sciences are concerned with knowledge of and in the decision process of the public and civic order." The definition is a powerful and important one because it contains the perspective of revolutionary science. With this definition Lasswell has generated two tasks for the field: first is the work of the social scientist in developing an analysis of the decision process; and second is the description of the role that social science knowledge plays in the decision process. Knowledge of the decision process suggests systematic, empirical analyses of how policies are made and implemented. Having a role in the decision process implies that the social scientist can and should provide relevant knowledge to the decision makers.

In other words, the social scientist has to anticipate and provide useful knowledge for policies attempting to solve such problems as poverty, crime, energy, family planning, and so forth.

Although the terms will be dealt with later, it is necessary to comment at this point on the juxtaposition of policy and science in the term policy sciences. Policy simply means a cluster of decisions with a particular purpose and audience in mind.

Science is a bit more troublesome to define because of its many connotations and myths. To many, science is "value-free." Immediately one sees the paradox between policy that has a particular purpose or end it is following (value-oriented) and science that is "neutral." Whether science is value-free is not an argument I wish to take up here. I am convinced the history of science reveals it to be full of such values as jealously and greed. I have argued this point in other chapters and would simply refer the reader to James D. Watson's The Double Helix for the humanistic side of science.

The term science is used because it implies the use of empirical data gathered from systematic observation. In other words, the use of the scientific method for improved policy making is crucial to the policy scientist. Obviously, the policy scientist has to train himself to be objective when analyzing a complex problem or his perceptions, observations, and recommendations will be weakened. But the basic point for the policy scientist is that objectivity is not the same thing as neutrality.

Finally the plural form of the noun, sciences, is used to stress the interdisciplinary nature of policy sciences. Complex problems require the expertise of many disciplines and scientists. The policy science approach based on the context of the social problem must incorporate a synthesis of techniques and bodies of knowledge. The effective policy scientist must command a battery of empirical skills in his assault on complexity. It is the use of empirical techniques (scientific) that separates the policy scientist professional from the flag-waving radical. Lasswell describes the former rather well: "As a professional man, who shares the scientist's disciplined concern for the empirical, he is searching for an optimum synthesis of the diverse skills that contribute to a dependable theory and practice of problem solving in the public interest."

Of course, the achievement of this is not easy and that is why the emphasis in Chapters 2 and 3 on General Systems Theory and communication. If policy scientists, trained in different disciplines, say sociology and law, are going to share knowledge on welfare reform, they need an intellectual framework as provided by GST to guide them. Quite clearly, they also need to be able to communicate. A communicative gestalt of the complexity must be apparent. The time dimension of the problem does not permit them to go back and acquire each other's expertise—they must be able to communicate about the problem and its proposed solutions now.

With policy sciences, a synergetic relationship between scientists of different disciplines must be established. Traditional disciplines such as the social and behavioral sciences can provide the basic training and body of knowledge (empirical data to some extent) for policy sciences. Policy sciences on the other hand can stimulate parts of the traditional social sciences to engage in more relevant policy-making activities.

AIMS OF POLICY SCIENCES

The aim of policy sciences is to solve societal problems. As Dror in his seminal work, Design for Policy Sciences (1971), states the aim, policy sciences are mainly concerned with improving policy making on the basis of systematic knowledge and structural rationality. Dror goes on to say that policy sciences are in principle "instrumental-normative," in the sense of being concerned with means and intermediate goals, rather than absolute values.

An obvious aim is to use science, more precisely the scientific method, to effect better policy making. Our body of scientific knowledge advanced because scientists were allowed to construct highly abstract theories far removed from the everyday world. Such work has been termed "basic research."

However, in the last two decades we have been confronted with a new set of problems, largely social and environmental in structure. We have concluded that it makes a great deal of sense to try to solve these problems with empirical knowledge. Generally we have called such efforts "applied research."

The aims of policy sciences follow the last scientific rubric but are actually much broader in scope. Policy sciences, for example, would likely address large societal issues like urban decay, race relations, poverty, and so on, while the applied research scientist would study more specific concrete problems like how to extract oil from the ocean floor or improve day care centers.

This would suggest that an objective of policy sciences is a form of research (inquiry) that produces empirical knowledge that is useful toward solving a policy problem. This means that the body of knowledge produced by the policy sciences must undergo the demands of any scientific knowledge: Conclusions are based on objective empirical data subject to public comment and review.

Certainly implicit in all of this is the aim for the field to behave like a scientific discipline, yet be flexible enough to abandon old and create new tools for improving policy making. This is crucial to the policy sciences growth because most people have little interest in the pursuit of knowledge as an end in itself. For some time now, scholars and policy makers with foresight have known that our contemporary problems require holistic, interdisciplinary approaches, but it has taken the real world of crises to force this view on the others. Most textbooks have little to say about the process of persuading others to recognize a societal problem.

Finally policy sciences aims at being normative in the utilization of its knowledge. It intends to tell policy makers what or how or when to improve their policies through recommendations based on empirical data.

Thus the aims of policy sciences suggest a different and until now an underdeveloped role for knowledge. How this is done is now the topic for the next section.

RESEARCH STYLE

Archibald (1970) has distinguished three types of orientation to social science utilization: the academic, the clinical, and the strategic. Researchers in the first group generate knowledge and leave it to others as to how to utilize it. The clinical researcher treats the client like a patient who needs his expertise as, say, a computer scientist showing an administrator how to best use software. The strategist views the client more as a partner or colleague who wants to mix his own practical knowledge with the more systematic approach of his adviser. The research style of the policy scientist is much like that of the strategic orientation.

In terms of methodological approach, the research style is different in substance and philosophy from that ordinarily used in conventional scientific research. The stimulus for this unconventional philosophy stems from the belief that novel problems require novel approaches. As Scott and Shore (1974) observe, "The use of conventional academic research and teaching modes, and their logical extension in the form of consultation on policy problems, cannot, we believe, generate the kind of information and knowledge that can be effectively used in social policy formulation."

Given the severity of our problems it seems that our best minds should be engaged in order to discover solutions. The age is gone when academics merely work on narrow but extremely technical problems if we are to avoid the criticisms leveled at social scientists as noted in Chapter 1.

In the academic world there is a tradition that to undertake research for a client—much less for pay—is to sell one's soul to the devil. Policy scientists, and perhaps it is fortunate that many of them work in think-tanks, obviously do not share this viewpoint and really believe that the growing body of social science knowledge should be applied to the solution of some of the chronic problems of our time. After all, the final goal of social science is a scientific explanation and prediction of human behavior in all settings.

As noted earlier, in the policy sciences knowledge has a different role to play. In traditional social science the worth of a bit of knowledge was in its precision, but in policy sciences the utilization of knowledge may not depend on its precision. The Cuban missile crisis offers a grim reminder of how bits of information were pieced together to reach deadly conclusions. Or, as Coleman (1972) points out, "[For] policy research, partial information available at the time an action must be taken is better than complete information after the time." And "the criteria of parsimony and elegance applied in discipline research are not important; the correctness of the prediction or results is important, and redundancy is valuable."

Knowledge in its new role in the policy sciences becomes a powerful tool for causing and manipulating change via policies. The policy scientist is concerned with discovering those independent variables that are subject to control. The reason is clear. If the policy maker is going to make any changes, he needs a lever. Through knowledge the policy scientist can discover the lever. Freeman (1963) notes this when he observes, "For the most part . . . the control, modification, and initiation of programs are functions of the policy system. One reasonably safe observation is that the policy system is least concerned about attitudinal phenomena and most concerned with behavioral ones; consequently, the latter have greater potential."

Thus the role of knowledge is tied to manipulation and control in policy sciences research. Let me quickly add here that one is not talking about manipulation and control as is used in narrow laboratory experiments. Because of the lack of external validity such research has little payoff in the policy sciences. In fact such research may go a long way toward explicating phenomena but offer no useful policy advice.

After proper description of the problem area, the major task of the policy scientist is to identify those policy-relevant variables that are subject to manipulation and control via the policy or program at hand. An example may clarify the point. In family planning and population control, variables that can be manipulated or controlled include attitudes toward contraceptives, what types can be obtained, and their availability. These three variables can be controlled to a reasonable extent by the family planning program. A variable outside the control of the program would be official church positions toward the use of contraceptives.

This issue of manipulation and control of policy-relevant variables reveals subtle but powerful differences between academic and policy sciences methods of measuring variables. Academic measures, concerned with reliability and validity, rely on goodness of fit and variance in the dependent variable while policy sciences measures stress program choices. In the final analysis this may mean very few variables are subject to control or manipulation in the policy program. In the real world this may offer a rather grim view of reality to the beleagured policy maker, particularly if the choices amount to "slim" and "none." However, as Novick (1973) concludes, "More resources are wasted doing the wrong things efficiently than can ever be wasted doing the right things inefficiently." Or as Cutt (1975) notes, "In such a quest it is better to be approximately right than precisely wrong."

Nevertheless there is a basis for hope. Economics, long a historical and social discipline before it became more behavioral, owes its recent status to the fact that its manipulative variables have been identified. Feuer (1954) argues that Keynesian models provided economics with this ability: "Keynesian ideas have been accepted not because they explained more than others but because they provided a set of causal laws whose independent variables are accessible to action in the present."

Thus the role of knowledge in policy sciences is not so much to collect facts or to make precise predictions as it is to offer other contributions to the policy process. While normative in approach, it does attempt to identify those program variables subject to manipulation and control, and in this process it helps to make concepts implicit and assumptions explicit. By singling out the important independent variables, limits can be placed on the range of possible outcomes and policy-maker judgments can be systematically examined and their effects tested. The value of the policy scientist's work lies not so much in the answers he provides but in the clarity of his arguments. The policy scientist does not seek to replace intuition and experience (attributes it is assumed the policy maker has) but through his analysis aims at enriching and broadening them—in other words, to extend the policy maker's capacity for judgment. The emphasis should be the process of thinking from which stems the answer. One of the best "answers" any policy scientist can provide for the policy maker is the generation of a new way of looking at the problem leading to a more adequate description of it.

METHODOLOGICAL ASSUMPTIONS

From the policy sciences literature one can extract several key methodological assumptions that guide policy sciences work. First, there is a strong reliance on GST and systems thinking. This dependence is not surprising since the world of policy is often a web of interdependent factors. Quite simply this means if a problem is complicated, then any effort to produce policies for dealing with it will require a strategy for taking into account all of the factors and their interactions at work. In addition, a systems perspective also provides the policy scientist with relevant analogies from other disciplines. Ideas from theoretical biology or computer science may suggest an analogy that helps to illuminate the problem. And Dror (1971) offers medicine as a helpful analogue for policy sciences development.

An important benefit or outcome of the systems approach may be to increase communication between social scientists and policy makers. Dror's position isclear. He feels that social scientists should be more interested in applying their knowledge to real-world problems, that policy makers should learn more about the knowledge of the social sciences, and that understanding and professional respect should be improved between the two groups. In other words, both systems need each other, or as Dror says it, "What is required is not some incremental change here or there, but far-reaching redesign in the two relevant systems and their interchanges."

Second is the broad macroperspective. As noted in earlier chapters, a holistic methodological stance is necessary for coping with complex social problems. In fact, something approaching a gestalt of the problem is required if meaningful policies are to be offered. In practice, this means taking a broad view of the difficulty and then trying to generate preferable solutions among several alternatives without being limited to cosmetic changes.

The point here is that to effectively use policy sciences, the analyst must avoid the trap of narrow or microapproaches. A microanalysis, while rich in details, is largely helpless when forced to deal with a complex issue like a national environmental policy. In a microstudy the scope is not broad enough to cope with all of the relevant variables. What is lacking, to use Vickers' (1965) apt phrase, is a "frame of appreciation."

The relation between macro- and microstudies is a difficult methodological problem for the policy scientist. Any researcher feels at home with his particular unit of analysis—the personality, a small group, the firm, a social class, national institutions—depending on his discipline. But the policy scientist must leave his home base and face reality. To study in some detail all of the hundreds or thousands of microunits that make up the macrounit (say, welfare reform) is obviously a task that would overwhelm any individual. To some extent there must be a blending of the two so that effective policies can be realized, and this has been done with some success in economics. As a discipline it has integrated analyses of the firm with macroissues like money supply, gross national product, and so forth.

Using this interdisciplinary approach I believe policy sciences, as a field of inquiry, is headed in the right direction. In particular I think this is achieved with the field's focus on decision theory. Using decision as a construct I believe there are some hopeful signs that this may function as a bridge between micro- and macrostudies. Thus decision making and related theory become our third methodological assumption. I use the term assumption here in the sense that the construct is assumed to offer payoff for the policy scientist. In the past few decades much effort has gone into the analysis of decision making. Despite the efforts of such areas as information theory, game theory, and some sophisticated math modeling, we still have little solid knowledge. Our theoretical constructs still fail by a wide margin to capture what happens in the decision-making process. And perhaps even more important, decision theory often fails to predict reasonably clear distinctions between outcomes based on policy options. In other words, the decision maker's uncertainty is not reduced if we tell him, "There are four options, each with a probability of success at 25 percent." The deficiency stems from a concentration on analytic rather than empirical knowledge. A theoretic framework is needed to close the gap between personal accounts of decision making and highly abstract models. Perhaps Dror's suggestion of medicine as a proper analogue for policy sciences would be helpful since it is a body of knowledge that has grown both from trial and error and scientific advances.

Despite the difficulties of decision theory it does seem too useful and germane to policy sciences to be cast aside. If it can be made to be more empirical rather than analytic, and some of the methodologies that follow in later chapters along with others seem to suggest this, then it must remain a key concept for policy sciences.

Fourth, there is an emphasis on description. Naturally this comes from the earlier focus on GST and macroanalyses. No small portion of the difficulty in solving complex problems lies in our inability to describe them as they are. Being human, our descriptions are based on perceptions. If we ask the "experts" to describe poverty we get many different answers. An economist offers one perspective, a sociologist another, while a welfare worker offers still another. The issue becomes even more complicated when we realize all three are correct. Consequently, the question "What is poverty?" requires complete description if we are to have any success in generating adequate policy. Obviously, the policy sciences must devote a major effort toward description. Our mass media are full of examples of policies that failed simply because the problem was never adequately described. An adequate description thus becomes the necessary condition for discovering effective policies.

Fifth, there is a definite futures perspective. It is clear that policies are designed to solve current problems in some future time period. In a general sense, policies function much like preventive medicine—if we do this now, we can lessen or avoid future problems. In some ways it is useful to view time as an independent variable in policy sciences research since the present represents a link between the past (antecedent conditions) and the future. Historical events or conditions are important to the policy scientist as trends or patterns may be discovered. Following this discovery future policies can be formed—with of course taking into consideration how these will change over time. Effective policies thus are made from past and future events or expected conditions. This can be demonstrated in an empirical way. Many practicing policy scientists were trained in or worked at think-tanks, such as Rand, where futures research methods like the Delphi technique and cross-impact analysis were developed. Futures research, an extension of policy sciences, and the related methodologies, Delphi and cross-impact analysis, will be discussed at length in later chapters (see Chapters 5, 8, and 9).

POLICY SCIENCES TRAINING

The teaching and training of people for a profession is a serious and difficult undertaking. This is truer of the policy sciences, for the difficulty of the subject matter and the serious consequences of policies designed to improve the social welfare.

Traditionally the training of policy scientists has been done more or less unknowingly by colleges and universities. Generally they have trained the student in one discipline, and years later we find that student making policy. Whether he is good at it depends largely on his own genius rather than on his college education. This is not unexpected, for universities are concerned with knowledge generation and enlightenment, while the world of work requires knowledge utilization. Annual surveys usually reveal this gap when working professionals are asked to compare their college preparation with their current duties.

Faced with this inadequate preparation of policy scientists, and the increased demand for someone so skilled, a number of research and development organizations (think-tanks) have begun in-house training of their own personnel. The pressure to do this has increased because of a related development in R&D work. Many clients are now demanding in their contracts that the R&D firm research the problem, make recommendations for solving it, and finally see that these are implemented. I personally worked on a state project in which my contract called for me to get the recommendations (in this case large amounts of funding) through the state legislature. I spent one year studying the problem from an economic perspective and then six additional months developing a communication strategy to persuade the legislature. If this trend toward guaranteed implementation continues (and I believe it will), traditional college training is inadequate.

As a result many R&D firms allow or require their employees to attend in-house seminars and workshops on "effective policy making," which are usually taught by their more experienced management or outside experts.

Recently a new development emerged. The Rand Corporation, the most well-known of the think-tanks, began to offer the Ph.D. in policy sciences. The Rand doctorate is certified by the state of California and a number of Ph.D.s have been awarded since 1974. A Rand spokesman said they had to begin offering the degree because the demand for policy scientists was so high and the universities were not offering the degree.

Rand's sense of the demand for well-trained policy scientists follows another interesting development among students. Paradoxically, the widespread disillusionment with government has not deterred a large number of students from planning careers in public service. I think this trend reflects a strong desire on the part of the students to make government work.

Some universities are sensitive to this large demand and have begun to offer specialized training in public policy. These programs among others can now be found at: the universities of California (Berkeley), Texas, Michigan, and Southern California; Carnegie-Mellon, Harvard, Stanford, and Duke universities. The curriculum usually offers a blend of the social and management sciences in training students to analyze and manage the complex problems of policy making in the government. They usually emphasize concepts and theories from the social and behavioral sciences and quantitative techniques, such as cost-benefit studies, cost-effectiveness measures, mathematical modeling and statistics. Some programs include ideas from the management sciences, such as organizational and decision theory.

Some of the learning techniques are almost revolutionary—in the Kuhn sense of the term. For example, at Harvard's John F. Kennedy School of Government, students are taught to look at a problem, take it apart, fill in the information gaps, make recommendations, and argue a viewpoint. Similar to Harvard's Business School, the Kennedy program utilizes the case study as the principal teaching tool. Students might well simulate the staff of a governmental agency in dealing with a particular problem. Berkeley's Graduate School of Public Policy stresses a pragmatic, "can-do" approach to public policy problems, sometimes requiring students to prepare 48-hour analyses as well as a major research project. The learning objective or theory is that the acquisition of technical competence is not as important as the ability to conceptualize a problem, find an appropriate model for it, and come up with useful advice. A special effort is made to see that students do not lose sight of the political realities and restraints in their recommendations. At the University of Texas' Lyndon B. Johnson School of Public Affairs, students gain practical experience in public policy making by serving as interns in various city, state, and federal government agencies. Sometimes students may actually spend a year working inside a department on a real-world problem.

Most of these programs are housed in professional schools, and the chief difference between them and traditional academic departments is that they emphasize problem-solving through a multidisciplinary approach. Some of them allow their students to pursue joint degrees, usually in law. Students are usually not planning to follow their traditional classmates and enter university teaching. Many of them say they plan to change jobs several times and work on different problems among various levels of government. Up until now graduates have had no trouble finding jobs, usually with planning and evaluation staffs of federal and state agencies. About a third of the graduates of the LBJ School have been hired by the State of Texas and many others have gone to work for private firms (often R&D) that do contractual research for governmental departments.

It is my conclusion that I would like future policy scientists trained in an academic atmosphere. Ideally I would like to see training take place in a school of policy sciences, but if university resources do not permit this then policy sciences should be part of the main core of curriculum in all professional schools. I think the degree objective should be the Ph.D. in policy sciences. The degree program should be two years of formal study with the third and final year devoted to working out in the field and completing the dissertation. Certainly I would like policy sciences courses available to undergraduates, but I think the complexity of real-world problems requires the rigorous training of the doctoral degree. I would think that the "typical" policy sciences student would have a degree in a traditional, well-established discipline. Based on this preformal training the policy sciences benefit from a broad-based body of knowledge so necessary to any multidisciplinary effort. The objectives of the doctoral program would be the learning, research, and application of policy sciences. As for employment, the students would be trained as professionals and would be expected to take positions involving policy making in public policy-making institutions. The curriculum for achieving this would include some social science courses depending on the amount of previous training in this area, qualitative and quantitative measuring techniques, planning theory, evaluation models, budget accounting including planning, programming, budgeting systems (PPBS) and zero-based budgeting techniques, organizational theory, macroeconomics, and decision theory. As a result students should then have sufficient knowledge in three key areas of policy sciences: the development of policy theory, decision making and policy analysis, and institutional change.

The challenge of such professional training is the integration of specialized knowledge with broad policy concerns. The student needs to be allowed to specialize in one area more than others, say decision theory, but has got to remain a generalist to evaluate policy. And finally, the integration between academic learning and field experiences is no simple task. However, such integration is crucial. Many students are able to master the theoretical material with ease but show little aptitude for grasping communication strategies, political realities, or persuasion campaigns—the other side of the policy sciences coin. I think the best way for preparing students to meet both realities is to provide two types of learning environments—one done at the university in seminars, the other, on-the-job experiences out in the field. The end result, if we are lucky, is a professional in the policy sciences who is on the one hand a thinker, researcher, scholar, theorist, and on the other hand an administrator, manager, or person of action. As difficult as it is, there is no choice but to do it, for being a problem solver demands it.

POLICY SCIENCES AS A PROFESSION

As a profession policy sciences is young. For decades people have been making policy decisions in our public institutions with mixed results. A number of the policies were bad, but because of hard work by others, simpler problems, and less interdependence between problems and systems we managed to muddle through. Today given the complexity of modern problems an attempt to muddle through may lead to disaster. Let me cite a recent example where only a structure was involved—essentially a mechanistic problem rather than a much more complicated social or life one. In the fall of 1976 the 60-story John Hancock Tower opened five years behind schedule and $83 million over budget. The most troublesome area was the 13.5 acres of glass that covered the building. In high winds, as is typical in Boston, the glass shattered and fell to the street. When the glass started breaking in 1972, company officials dismissed it as routine construction damage. But eventually it became apparent the problem was wind, not workmen. So all 10,344 double panes of glass were removed and replaced with half-inch-thick single sheets. That policy mistake cost $7.5 million, and litigation over paying for the glass is expected to last for years. As the new sheets were being installed something had to be done about the broken ones. Workmen covered these with plywood patches and in Boston the building was known as the world's tallest plywood building. Meanwhile, the fire department, worried that the building was a fire hazard, ordered the plywood covered with black fire-resistant paint. When construction began it was estimated that it would cost $75 million and be ready by late 1971. The latest construction figure is $158 million. There have been other problems as well. Neighbors have complained that the tower, built on landfill, was causing the foundations of nearby buildings to shift. Later people noticed the building was swaying in the wind, so 1,500 tons of steel were installed in the elevator shafts and stairwells to steady it.

This problem in all its complexity is small compared to the things that could go wrong in welfare reform, energy, and pollution controls. At the moment the first mistakes and unexpected problems are beginning to come in on the Alaska pipeline. The point here is that the policy sciences professional must be prepared to deal with hopelessly complex issues—and the Hancock Building shows how often the "experts" are wrong.

Despite the quality of their advice there are a number of national indicators that social scientists have been and will increasingly be asked—at least up to the point where the answers are useful as was pointed out in Chapter 1—by policy makers to help them in their decisions. These indicators of usage indicate that a relationship exists between buyers and sellers of information. Social scientists/policy scientists are believed to have or to be able to generate a scarce commodity information. As long as this view prevails, the profession of policy sciences should grow. This relationship is based on economic activity—an exchange of money for information. An indication of the growth of the profession would be to look at the data on the number of social scientists involved in the policy process, the amount of money spent, and where these professionals are employed. This has been done in a highly important and significant work by Horowitz and Katz (1975). They conclude that the rate of growth in federal support for human resources has approximately doubled every three years for the last 12 years. They note that the shift in federal spending from defense and space to human resources should mean more R&D funds are available to social scientists than in any other time period. Consequently more social science/policy science positions are available in applied programs, "signifying a shift from an academic to a policy-oriented work life for social scientists." Horowitz and Katz conclude: "All of this adds up to growth in the size and power of the social science profession leading to a still greater impact by the social scientific community on policy construction, implementation and evaluation." It is important to point out to the reader that although the social sciences still receive the smallest amount of federal funds, they are the fastest growing, now reflecting a significant percent of federal outlays for research. Consequently the issue is no longer some small level of expenditures for social sciences as has always been true in the past, but one of a large and important priority that raises profound implications and considerations for the profession of policy sciences. To this Horowitz and Katz add that the social sciences have been transformed "from a small, ancillary activity performed behind university walls to a large-scale, central service performed in the full view of the body politic."

It is important to pause here for a moment and offer some specific examples of this transformation. In hearings before the Senate Government Operations Committee (1968, 322-33) Senator Walter Mondale described one of the objectives of the Full Opportunity and Social Accounting Act (Senate 5: Title 1): "formation of the Council of Social Advisors, which advisory council to the President would draw from disciplines of social science in analyzing and evaluating progress in social reform." The idea was that a council of social advisers would be of much help to the president in identifying needs, establishing priorities, and evaluating programs, and it would produce much-needed information for policy makers in such areas as education, welfare, job training, health care, and antipoverty programs.

In 1966 and 1967 Senator Fred Harris, chairman of the Subcommittee on Government Research of the Senate Committee on Government Operations, proposed that a national foundation for the social sciences be established. The director of the National Science Foundation (NSF) opposed the creation of a separate foundation and much opposition came from Herbert Simon, a political scientist and psychologist from Carnegie-Mellon University. His position was that out of scientific and practical necessity there was only the need for a single scientific organization, NSF. Given this opposition and the restrictions on spending due to the Vietnam War there was little hope for the passage of the bill, and despite the cosponsorship of 32 senators the bill was not enacted.

Despite the failure, the Harris bill seemed to awaken many of those in the federal government to the need for an increased role on the part of the social sciences in policy making. For example, the Office of Technology Assessment, established in 1972 with an emphasis on the physical sciences, has recognized the necessity of social scientists to meeting its duties, such as: economists and public policy analysts to upgrade the quality of the environment; sociologists and public opinion specialists to investigate social and attitudinal obstacles to food irradiation and the causes of these obstacles; consumer analysts to study wastepaper recycling; urban planners to look at possible use of geothermal energy; experimental psychologists, energy economists, and political scientists to analyze breeder reactor implications; experimental and social psychologists to study automotive air bags; others in economics, political science, and international affairs to study nuclear-materials safeguards; and sociologists, economists, health care administrators, population statisticians, and demographers to examine genetic engineering.

As Horowitz and Katz conclude, "Nonetheless, legislative relief or not, budgetary allocations for social scientists went soaring and thus relieved any great pressure for new congressional measures. What could not be accomplished through the act of Congress could clearly be achieved through the Bureau of the Budget."

Recently social scientists have found their way indirectly into the executive office, sometimes through direct appointment as with Kissinger, Moynihan, and Schultz. In the Carter administration, Secretary of Labor Marshall was a former economics professor at the University of Texas.

Most but not all social scientists/policy scientists establish careers in government. The National Science Foundation estimates that approximately 5 percent of all social scientists who have their doctoral degrees are employed in private industry. General Motors (GM) offers an illustration of how social scientists are employed in private industry for purposes of policy research. GM has a Societal Analysis Department that functions as a long-range planning arm for the auto manufacturer. Ford Motor Company, General Electric, and Bell Laboratories conduct planning research similar to GM's. As concerns mount over energy conservation/consumption and pollution, social science factors must enter into more corporate policy efforts.

Finally the policy sciences profession is playing a larger role in the judicial system. In a number of important cases the courts have used social science information to decide legal issues affecting the public welfare. This has been particularly true in cases involving race relations as in Brown v. Board of Education and most recently in the selection of jurors.

From this brief survey I think it is safe to conclude that policy sciences as a young profession is growing with even greater demand for its professionals in the future.

BARRIERS TO POLICY SCIENCES

There appear to be two barriers to the complete adoption of policy sciences as an aid to effective policy making. The first has been identified and commented on at length by Dror (1971) and will be summarized here. Dror argues that the strong resistance of the science community to changes in the basic paradigms of science and in the disciplinary structure of scientific activity is a formidable barrier. The research style and assumptions of the policy sciences, which were presented earlier in this chapter, reveal why traditional science stands as a strong barrier to policy sciences.

Dror concludes that universities offer a rather inhospitable environment for policy research organizations:

the tight compartmental structure, which inhibits interdisciplinary and even multidisciplinary endeavors; the distance
from policymaking reality, which inhibits policy relevant
research; traditions of academic scholarship on the lines
of the paradigms of normal sciences and research; rules
patterns and incentive structures for academic staff, which
reward scientific conservatism and penalize innovation . . .
and more and more—the necessity to devote all one's time
to teaching and the tradition of publication, habits of in-
fighting and internal politics.

Dror makes a strong case here, and one that does have considerable merit. As Alexis de Tocqueville commented on French intel-
lectuals of the prerevolutionary period: "Their very way of living
led these writers to indulge in abstract theories and generalizations
regarding the nature of government, and to place a blind confidence
in these. For living as they did, quite out of touch with practical
politics, they lacked the experience which might have tempered their
enthusiasm."
    If one barrier lies on the supply side the other lies on the demand
side. There is a tendency on the part of many policy makers, especially in the federal government, not to use social science findings in
their decision making. Caplan (1976) found in his study of 204 high-
level federal policy makers that there is a high level of interest in and
receptivity to social science information but little evidence that such
information actually enters into the decision-making activity. Caplan's
important study presents us with something of a paradox: it would
appear that policy makers express an eagerness to get all the policy-
relevant scientific information they can, and yet they are not influ-
enced by such information if they receive it. Caplan's data suggest
some reasons why social science information does not impact on the
policy-making process: social scientists conceive of complex social
problems only in the limited terms of their own discipline; an over-
reliance on quantitative methods; social science research is focused
on understanding and fails to provide an action-framework necessary
for problem solving. Caplan goes on to offer an argument similar to
C. P. Snow's in The Two Cultures in which he explains the gap between
the humanities and the hard sciences. It is argued that social scientists and policy makers live in separate worlds with different and often
conflicting values, different reward systems, and different languages.
    The study also revealed that information is usually rejected for
one of three reasons: either the policy maker does not believe the
data on grounds of objectivity, or the findings are counterintuitive,
or the data is accepted as valid but the information is rejected because
it is politically infeasible to utilize it. Perhaps this led Caplan to

comment that governmental decision making was like sausage making: "When you see what goes into it, you lose your appetite."

Finally Caplan's data suggest that most policy makers could be classified into three information-processing styles: the clinical orientation—the most active users of scientific information gather information and then consider its policy implications given existing social and political constraints; the academic orientation—this group uses scientific information in moderate amounts and focuses almost exclusively on the diagnosis or internal logic of problems; the advocacy orientation—the users, often lawyers, utilize only that part of the information that fits with political realities.

Certainly this is a powerful barrier to the spread of policy sciences, but one, I believe, that can be overcome. The early arguments for policy sciences and the inherent differences between it and traditional science as pointed out in the first part of this chapter suggest strategies and routes for overcoming this barrier. The objections of policy makers as to why they do not use social science research findings mirror the intrinsic beginnings of policy sciences. Policy scientists recognize both barriers and are working to transcend them: This is why policy sciences has emerged as a new intellectual field based on novel scientific paradigms.

FINAL CONSIDERATIONS

As noted earlier in this chapter, knowledge plays a unique role in policy sciences. It takes on the role of advocate. This is in contrast to the useful but narrow role of the mere accumulation of information. Orlans (1975) captures the spirit of this notion rather well with his comment, "It is easier to increase the volume of information, to observe and record almost any event in almost any detail, than to use that information in any way: even to read, let alone retain or act upon it."

Even when we try to act upon it our policies may backfire in our face. Let me cite a true and ironic example. As of this writing northern California is experiencing a severe drought. The City of San Francisco implemented a water-rationing policy based largely on personal conservation. The policy of conservation worked—in fact, it worked too well. Recently San Franciscans were warned by city officials that, despite rationing, if they do not start using more water they are in for a hefty rate increase.

One city official explained the contradiction in the policy. The reason for the threatened increase is that the public was "overzealous" in cutting back on its water usage to the point that the city Water Department is faced with a severe loss in revenue. In other words, if you sell less water you have less money.

Apparently the city policy makers had counted on reducing water consumption only 25 percent, but the actual consumption was down to 40 percent. The policy thus produced a "Catch-22" type of problem: an attempt to keep people convinced of the seriousness of the drought on the one hand while encouraging them to use more water on the other.

What went wrong with the policy was that it was developed in too narrow a context with little thought given to future events. Short-sighted pragmatism often tends to lose sight of the social context that results in short-lasting policies. It also reveals a lack of appreciation for the communicative aspects of any policy. If we define communication as behavior, then all acts are communicative. As Vickers (1973) pointedly observes, "Even the bomb at Hiroshima was, and was intended to be, more effective as a communication than as an agent of destruction."

Since communication permeates every facet of a person's behavior, the study of communication is no less than one way to study policy making. Communication is a useful concept precisely because it is one more handle whereby we can effectively study policy making. Communication is one of those few fundamental variables through which any policy decision is dependent. Certainly in the San Francisco example the policy makers forgot the persuasive impact of communication on the citizenry. As the social sciences move from behind the walls of academia to the arena of action the communication between policy scientists and policy makers becomes crucial. It is interesting to note the large number of books written for business managers by academics and consultants while there are practically none for public policy makers.

For many traditionally trained social scientists, the role of knowledge as advocate leads them into the uncomfortable waters of prescription and normativism. This is a role scientists have debated for years, and I will not attempt to resolve it here. My position is fairly clear on the issue, but I would like to point out that there is a rich history of scientists' prescribing for the betterment of society. Certainly the field of medicine offers a fruitful model in which scientific knowledge and method is put to use to cure the ills of the sick. A social scientist is no more apt to violate his professional standards while performing his science than is a physician his oath. The objective is to improve policy making, and the social scientist functioning as a policy scientist must realize that his role of advocate can often make a difference in the effectiveness of the policy. As a policy scientist/social scientist he has his own norms and values and these are somewhat different from those of the policy maker because the realities of their respective roles are different. Beyond this, the policy scientist can do much to shape the norms and values from which his policy is made. Vickers (1973) is particularly lucid on this theme:

What we want and do not want to do is limited and often
transformed not only by what we can and cannot do, but
also by what we must and must not do, where those words
are used of social obligation in the widest sense, and also
by what we ought and ought not to do. . . . It would be
strange if the verbs which distinguish these changes did
not correspond with some psychological realities.

Garry D. Brewer, editor of Policy Sciences (1974), makes the
same point in a different way: "There is the unstinting demand to behave as scientists, and to the greatest extent possible use, modify and
create new tools, techniques and explanations to understand as well
as possible what impedes and supports the realization of better policies—purposive acts taken on society's behalf."

To do this policy sciences requires two acts of translation as
suggested by Coleman (1972): first, the translation of the problem
from the world of reality and policy into the world of scientific method,
and then a translation of the research results back into the world of
reality and policy.

Lewin and Shakun (1976) offer some particularly useful insights
for doing this through their construct, "situational normativism."
To oversimplify, situational normativism attempts to take the components of policy sciences and put them to work effectively on real decision problems. The approach is situational in that each problem
must be approached individually, but the methodology is generally
heuristic. According to Lewin and Shakun this involves a synthesis
of descriptive (behavioral) and normative approaches. The analysis
begins with a descriptive model of a real-world decision situation including the participants, their values, and the decision rules that determine existing outcomes. Then the analysis turns normative in
that prescribed alternatives are presented. In addition, constraints
like implementation and political feasibility have to be dealt with.

The real art of policy sciences is to shift from an incomplete description of the problem to a position of understanding that allows one
to offer workable solutions; this is similar to the translation notion of
Coleman. This means that the policy scientist must cope with uncertainty, a troublesome aspect of policy making, but one that must be
recognized. It is realistic to say that major policy decisions must often be made under uncertain conditions, and this means that the policy
maker is operating in a subjective mode—an issue is decided by a
matter of choice. Any social problem is characterized by elements
that are unknown or uncertain and will remain so. However, the objective is to try to shift the system from "pure uncertainty" where
outcomes can be predicted, but one cannot give any probability statements for them. And this is where the social scientist/policy scien-

tist who is familiar with working with uncertain variables in a probabilistic sense can be of much use to the policy maker.

This can be done in two traditional ways. One can assign probabilities to outcomes on an a priori basis as, say, 50-50 in the heads
and tails of a coin. Or one can assign probabilities based on previous
observations of outcomes. In short, both methods assign or specify
the uncertainty in probabilities. Consider this example: Suppose
one has a sack full of colored marbles and plans to roll them down a
slide. The objective is to predict the final distribution of the marbles. Probabilities could be assigned based on the a priori method,
but this would mean fairly sophisticated mathematics and precise
measurements. Or the second method could be used: actually perform the experiment several times, observe the distribution, and
then use statistical inference to estimate the frequency probabilities
of each marble.

This simple little example would work if living systems were
not so complex, but social problems are hopelessly so. What do we
do, say, for constructing an energy policy over the next five years?
The first two methods are impractical. The neo-Bayesian school offers a solution: Simply estimate the necessary probabilities in a more
or less educated manner. A policy maker has little choice but the
third method, for he cannot predict the behavior of social elements
with the necessary precision (as required in the first method) of the
laws of mechanics, and the second requires the repetition and controls
of the laboratory. So the policy maker accepts this reality and assigns
or guesses probability estimates of uncertainty. Such is the reality
of the policy maker. This means he must look to future events and
make some estimate of the probability of their occurrence. Thanks
to policy sciences he need not make these estimates alone. Policy
sciences, through the use of specific methodologies, can add precision
to such estimates. Probability statements, while still subjective,
can be communicated to key policy makers with more precision so as
to avoid catastrophe. Such methods may keep the policy maker from
painting himself into a corner, as when one option is presented that
could be an attractive solution except that it is very risky. A better
set of options would be to have several alternatives that may work
with less risky certainty and can be implemented and changed over
time if they fail to work.

Dror (1971) offers a simple metaphor to illustrate the point:

Policy sciences theory states that one should not leave the
problem of crossing a river until the river is reached;
rather, one should survey the territory in advance, identify rivers flowing through it, decide whether it is at all
necessary to cross the river—and if so, where and how to

cross it—then prepare in advance the materials for crossing the river, and design a logistic network, so that the
material is ready when the river is reached.

Such a network is the purpose of the remaining chapters. Methodologies for solving complex social problems via policy sciences are
the topics for these chapters.

REFERENCES

Archibald, K. A. 1970. "Alternative Orientation to Social Science
Utilization." Social Science Information 9 (April).

Brewer, Garry. 1974. "Editorial." Policy Sciences 5.

Caplan, N. 1976. "Private Research and Public Policy: An Uncertain Marriage." Psychology Today, August.

Coleman, J. 1972. Policy Research in the Social Sciences. Morristown, N.J.: General Learning Press.

Cutt, J. 1975. "Policy Analysis: A Conceptual Base for a Theory of
Improvement." Policy Sciences 6.

Dror, Yehezkel. 1971. Design for Policy Sciences. New York: Elsevier.

Feuer, L. 1954. "Causality and Social Sciences." Journal of Philosophy 51 (November).

Freeman, H. 1963. "The Strategy of Social Policy Research." In
Social Welfare Reform. New York: Columbia University Press.

Horowitz, I., and J. Katz. 1975. Social Science and Public Policy
in the United States. New York: Praeger.

Lasswell, Harold. 1971. A Preview of Policy Sciences. New York:
Elsevier.

Lerner, Daniel, and Harold Lasswell, eds. 1951. The Policy
Sciences. Stanford, Calif.: Stanford University Press.

Lewin, A., and M. Shakun. 1976. "Situational Normativism: A Descriptive-Normative Approach to Decision Making and Policy Sciences." Policy Sciences 7.

Novick, D. 1973. Current Practice in Program Budgeting (PPBS). London: Heinemann.

Orlans, H. 1975. "Neutrality and Advocacy in Policy Research." Policy Sciences 6.

Scott, R., and A. Shore. 1974. "Sociology and Social Experimentation: Observations on the Application of Sociology to Applied Problems." Mathematica 4.

U.S. Congress, Senate, Government Operations Committee, Hearings, 1968.

Vickers, Sir Geoffrey. 1973. "Values, Norms and Policies." Policy Sciences 4.

5
Futures Research

Adlai Stevenson in his last speech in 1965 said, "We travel together on a little spaceship, dependent on its vulnerable supplies of air and soil" and since then the spaceship earth metaphor has become a symbol of how fragile life can be and how precarious the future.

It appears it has taken Alvin Toffler (1970) with his dramatic Future Shock to awaken the masses and to start them thinking about the future. Toffler's (1972) perception as a sage extended to the academic community when he observed,

> It is becoming acceptable, in academic circles, to talk
> about the future. (Before now it seemed unscholarly, unscien-
> tific, even "unserious.") Some of the new energies are
> spilling over into and influencing the social sciences, the
> humanities, and other disciplines, forcing them again and
> again to ask, "what are the hidden side effects, the long-
> range consequences of any action?"

Today there is empirical evidence that Toffler was right, to an extent, about academics' becoming concerned about the "future" as a concept worthy of research. A large number of professors are actively engaged in futures research, degree programs do exist, centers for futures research are functioning at universities, futures-oriented think-tanks have become part of the R&D community, various governments now have a futures component in their planning efforts, and there are scholarly publications dealing with the future.

WHAT IS FUTURES RESEARCH?

There is some difficulty in trying to define a concept that is constantly changing—much like trying to catch one's shadow as it keeps moving. Even though the field is hardly over a decade old, enough of a pattern exists for a partial definition to emerge.

I shall define futures research as any activity that improves our understanding about the future consequences of present decisions and policies. Inherent in this definition is the real locus of futures research: an examination of what can be rather than what will be or should be. Hence, the phrase, "inventing the future(s)" has become the motto of one seriously engaged in futures research. Futures research is not that concerned with predicting the future—an activity best left to fortune tellers—but is primarily concerned with discovering future consequences resulting from specific decisions or policies. If the coin is flipped over, this suggests that once we know the future we would like, we can go to work trying to figure out how to get there. In a simplified way, one may view futures research as long-range planning. Rather than asking who will be president in the year 2000, or what kind of automobiles will we drive, the futures researcher may be asking what percent of our daily consumption of oil will come from the Alaska pipeline.

Futures research can be broken down into three centers of activity: planning, forecasting, and decision making. In the early years of futures research, the field was dominated by a concern with technological forecasting. Considerable effort was spent on discovering the impact of technological breakthroughs on man and society. Predictions about the effects of NASA space technology, computers, transistors, and so on, were common and were usually conducted by natural scientists and engineers.

Today that emphasis has shifted more to the normative end of the spectrum with concerns about planning and decision making. Futures researchers have begun to explore the consequences, costs, alternative courses of action, goals, benefits, and options of particular policies. Much of this has been brought on by private industry and public institutions. Business has increasingly become aware of how changes in the social, economic, and technological environment vastly affect their profits. And in an age of accountability and limited natural resources, governments and nonprofit institutions have to know what kinds of services they will have to provide in the next decade. Planning and careful decision making thus become crucial.

WHY FUTURES RESEARCH?

All of us who are alive know that we live in an era of future shock, with change occurring with ever-increasing rapidity. Of course, Toffler has written of the consequences of this. Coupled with this development, our decisions concern increasingly complex phenomena. The fact that we do not decide very effectively is illustrated by the re-

ports of the daily news media. And when we have to extend that decision into the future, as in solving the energy crisis or dealing with
urban decay, we tend to do even more poorly.

As a reaction to this, many of our policies concentrate on a reactive type of decision making in order to correct for changes in the
system's immediate environment. It seems increasingly useful to
view the system's environment as an independent variable. Emery
and Trist (1965) have described our current situation as a "turbulent-
field" environment. Such surroundings are worse than uncertain ones
because under these conditions an organization is not aware of the
variables or their probabilities of occurrence affecting its very survival.

A system could be faced with a decision under conditions of certainty where the relevant variables are known and have probabilities
of either 0.0 or 1.0. A second set of conditions, risk, could exist
under which the system knows the probabilities lie between 0.0 and 1.
and can be calculated. In a condition of uncertainty, the system has
identified the variables but is unable to calculate their probabilities
of occurrence. But when the system is operating in a turbulent environment neither the relevant variables nor their probabilities have
been identified. Unfortunately, it is in this last set of conditions that
many systems today find themselves having to function. Consequently
rather than reactive decision making we need adaptive and inventive
policies. Often, a system's response to turbulent-field conditions is
reactive and most of these reactions tend to increase the general tur-
bulence. A frightening example is an arms race between nations in
which each increases its arsenal as a response to the other nation's
growing arms supplies. Regulation, not reaction, becomes the key
concept for policy making.

There are many reasons for turbulent-field environments, but
three important ones may be cited for now. First, there is an increase in the urgency of problems because we have little "lead time"
to solve them. The age of change does not give us the luxury of nine-
teenth-century America: time to watch events unfold before we act
on them. Second, today's problems do not occur in isolation but tend
to interact violently with each other. A nation's foreign affairs are
even more difficult to conduct because the world has turned into a
global village. Because of this interconnectedness of our problems,
it is increasingly difficult to take direct action because there is no
single cause and a short-run solution can actually make things worse
in the long run. Too often the policy maker is like the little Dutch boy
with not enough fingers to plug the dike. Third, there has been a failure of our old models and theories to cope adequately with space-age
problems. Most of the theories based on natural science principles
and Newtonian physics simply cannot grapple with today's complexity.

The old approaches, traditionally mechanistic in that systems could not change their internal structures, cannot explain or predict problems that are essentially dynamic and organismic. Economic forecasting is a good example. Most economic forecasts are based on econometric theories that are mechanistic, short term, and static, but such forecasts soon become unrealistic when applied to world economies. As never before, nations' economies are tied together, and we need new dynamic theory to explain, much less predict, them.

Today we have innumerable problems sufficiently complex and interconnected that solutions will require planning and policies that can be measured for the next five to 30 years. The problems are such that they cannot be solved overnight but will require efforts into the near future. Among these are insufficient supplies of energy, urban decay, pollution, crime and the inadequacy of the criminal justice system, inadequate health care, problems of race, unpredictable changes in the economy, poverty, housing shortages, mental health problems, the breakdown of the family, unemployment, invasions of privacy, uncontrolled technology, and inefficient government.

As you think back over these problems, notice how many of them are tied to one another and, because of their complexity, extend into the foreseeable future.

Not wanting to sound like Malthus, I do think there is a basis for hope. There seems to be an increased awareness that careful planning is the only way to attack complexity. NASA accomplishments and PPBS (despite its limitations) are current examples as well as an infinite number from business. Also, a growing appreciation for the interdependence among complex problems has led to a new level of acceptance for systemic thinking and explanation. New planning and analytical methods have been developed that provide the capability to foresee problems before they become crises. And finally there are technological and intellectual capabilities to create a hopeful future.

Obviously we live in an age of technology. Technological innovations do occur with astonishing rapidity and often do improve our standard of living. However, such accomplishments may come at a high price. Because technological advances always occur in some future time, it is relevant to explore the interaction between technology and society and to consider the need and role of futures research in this relationship. The 1960s were clearly years of technological innovations with dramatic developments in space, computers, and communications, and these years also saw technological procedures applied to social problems like health, education, and welfare with expected answers as found in NASA achievements. But getting to the moon proved a lot easier for the Kennedy administration than finding solutions to poverty as attempted by the Johnson administration's "Great Society." The 1960s also reveal some of the negative effects of technology. As so clearly illustrated by Amara (1975), technology tends to increase alienation for large segments of society by making so many choices available to individuals that they cannot adequately cope with their social environment. For example, the "pill" provided a woman with a choice about pregnancy but left her with health (harmful side effects) and religious (would the church allow it on moral grounds) questions.

Also technology has tended to isolate individuals rather than unite them on an interpersonal basis. The automobile and the television often have the effect of reducing communication among family members, and even the telephone, despite Ma Bell's advertising that it brings us together, has lessened such personal contacts as letter writing and meeting face to face.

Technology usually results in a concentration of wealth among technically advanced nations, adding to the potential (if not real) conflicts between the "have" and "have-not" nations.

Finally, technology concentrates power in big government and big corporations because only they have the resources and the assumed responsibility to make the commitment to technological advancement.

Today the technology debate rages between those who would stop technology and "return to the soil" and those who blindly believe technology can solve any technical or social problem. History teaches us better.

Thus, in planning for the future one of the great difficulties is to incorporate technological change into our projections and plans. One must remain aware that there are two edges to the technological sword. As Priban (1975) has observed, technology has progressed in three historical phases with man improving on what he has already accomplished in the first. In the second, new things are accomplished and in the third, man must change his lifestyle to match the opportunities now offered by technology. Today man is pushed and pulled into the world of computers and instant communications creating a new structure to society. Much of the current instability arises from an inability to regulate technology and recognize side effects (as in losses of privacy with computers and data banks). The trick is not simply to view a piece of technological hardware as an independent variable, but to realize that the final "state of the art" or set of conditions arises from the interaction of numerous factors.

Consequently, a forward analysis or "futures capability" is a necessary first step for developing plans and policies for attacking our problems and their related complexities. This cannot be done suddenly or easily. The price for purchasing a view of the future is rising. As noted previously, problems mount, lead time diminishes, the complexity increases, and the consequences become more dire. But the way forward can be charted and futures research can become our compass.

AIMS OF FUTURES RESEARCH

There is a great deal of folk wisdom suggesting that we are carried into the future by uncontrollable riptides and strong currents. This view seems unrealistic because the currents are man-made and therefore controllable.

Futures research attempts to change this old viewpoint by introducing the concept of alternative futures. The future is not a singular noun. In fact, the future is not one inescapable state, but actually is one of a multitude of possible futures. Bertrand de Jouvenel makes the same point rather dramatically with his term "futuribles."

The central theme of futures research is to broaden the concept from simple forecasting to one that attempts to explain the effects of various actions so that effective policies can be generated, thereby creating the future conditions deemed desirable. The point is that we can affect future outcomes, and policy makers as well as the citizenry must be made aware of this capability. Essentially one is offering a cybernetic view of life: through our actions we affect the environment which in turn affects us so that an evolving cycle is established. Now the direction and speed of this cycle cannot be corrected instantly and therefore must be anticipated. Such thinking necessitates developing a sense of direction and an understanding that actions have to be monitored and continuously modified. Also a systemic awareness of the reality we operate in is necessary. In short, a discovery is imperative that man has the power to shape his own future, or as Dennis Gabor (1964) has put it, "Till now, man has been up against Nature; from now on, he will be up against his own nature."

For any institution to become futures oriented, it must learn to operate on the assumption that its most valuable resource is the future. Because of this assumption, the institution can create its own future and adapt to change when necessary. In the late twentieth century the ability to change is probably the most important element to survival. In order to learn to use and control this resource, policy makers have to ground themselves in futures thinking. Several points seem necessary. First, futures research does not tell us what will happen, but instead tells us what will likely happen if something else happens. The "if" is the conditional qualifier. Second, the planning period is much greater in futures research than in traditional planning. Typical institutions, whether government or industry, usually think in one- to five-year plans. These are usually narrow in scope, concentrating on one problem or a single goal. But futures research considers a much longer time frame—say, ten to 30 years. These longer time periods are necessary if one is to grasp complicated problems and try to deal with them. For example, one cannot improve the harsh economic realities of the inner city in a one-year plan. To change so many of the variables that contribute to the economic state of the city ghetto requires careful planning and time for the policies to work.

Third, the future does not suddenly arrive at the doorstep in the form of the daily newspaper or a letter. The signs of what the future will look like are found in the present. The organization that finds itself in economic or legal difficulty must realize that there were antecedent conditions and early warning signals. The trick is to develop methods and procedures for picking up these early warning signals so that options for dealing with the coming changes can be developed. Implicit in this is the need to anticipate change rather than reacting to it after it has occurred. Most, if not all, knowledge about the future is derived by some form of extrapolation from the past.

To fully appreciate the importance of this anticipatory reorientation, a final aim must be spelled out. In making our projections about the future we assume we have accounted for all the possible outcomes, but in reality we know we can never be sure. So instead of concentrating on whether all the outcomes have been identified, futures research concentrates on generating as complete a list as possible. The methodologies of futures research must be oriented to uncovering outcomes that might be overlooked. Much of futures research is concerned with understanding what alternative futures are possible and what actions are necessary (along with the costs) for achieving them. In futures research much of the work rests on opinion, judgment, and speculation, so it is terribly important that our projections be derived systematically. How this can be done will be taken up later.

PRACTITIONERS OF FUTURES RESEARCH

Futures research, as an intellectual activity, is not much more than ten years old. There were some earlier foundations laid in the early 1960s by Bertrand de Jouvenel and his "Futuribles" group, Daniel Bell formed the Commission on the Year 2000, Dennis Gabor wrote "Inventing the Future," and Robert L. Heilbroner contributed his The Future as History in 1961. But these were simply seeds, for the full bloom of futures research began in the middle and late 1960s. Such publications included Herman Kahn and Anthony J. Wiener, The Year 2000 (1967), John Kenneth Galbraith, The New Industrial State (1967), Bertrand de Jouvenel, The Art of Conjecture (1967), Gordon R. Taylor, The Biological Time Bomb (1968), Don Fabun, The Dynamics of Change (1967), Erich Jantsch, Technological Forecasting in Perspective (1967), Olaf Helmer, T. Gordon, and B. Brown, Social Technology (1966), and Daniel Bell, ed., "Toward the Year 2000," Daedalus (1967). The particular efforts of the Futuribles group and Rand-sponsored research teams did much to give birth to worldwide futures studies and produced such offspring in the United States as the Educational Policy Research Centers and the Office of Technology Assessment.

I think it important here to take a slight pause and reflect in an overall fashion how the practitioners of futures research can be categorized. This seems necessary because futures research has produced a considerable amount of activity in one decade and has included some charlatans and incompetents along with serious researchers.

One overview is offered by Dror (1973), long-time writer and observer of futures research. He suggests that three different schools of futurists can be identified: predictors, utopians, and planners.

The predictive school, developed in the United States, has concentrated on forecasting futures primarily through such methods as technological, strategic, and social forecasting, as well as Delphi technique, cross-impact analysis, computer simulation, mathematical extrapolation, and scenario design. Much of this methodology was developed at the Rand Corporation, the Hudson Institute, and the Institute for the Future. Obviously the emphasis has been on sophisticated methodology.

The utopian school has focused its energy on inventing desirable futures. No single country accounts for this school, although much interest has centered in Europe.

Finally, the planning school aims for a utopian future but concentrates its efforts on designing policies that will achieve this particular future. This school depends on planning theory and policy sciences for its basic methodology. Advocates of this school can be found anywhere, but there has been a concentration in socialist countries.

Dror also offers another classification scheme. He divides futures research practitioners into two groups: activists and scholars. The first group, more political, seeks platforms in order to more actively shape the future and expound their particular ideologies.

The other group, the scholars, tends to concentrate on methodologies and techniques. Too often the problem with this group is that intellectual debate turns into inaction.

Futures research would be further advanced if the best of both groups could be combined. One cannot deny that our problems are large and complex enough that anyone wanting to change them must do so actively. Futures research is not a spectator sport. The scholars at some point must stop their long-winded debates over methodology and become advocates. They must offer advice, make predictions, and recommend to those with power and responsibility. A good guideline for doing this is offered by Beer in his Platform for Change (1975).

On the other hand, if futures research is going to accomplish anything, the activists are going to have to stop shouting at one another and listen to the offerings of the scholars. If they do this they may be surprised at what they find. Common sense and wishful thinking can contribute only so much toward solving complicated problems: sitting at the beach observing the waves can never lead to an explanation of tides. At some point the knowledge of physics must be applied to the sea, the earth, and the moon.

As the complexity of problems increases, the urgent need is for perceptive thinkers to be attracted to futures research, resulting in new ideas, better methodologies, and a greater rate of return from the discipline. Hopefully, synergetic interaction between the best of the two groups would advance the state of the art. What is not useful should be dropped, or as Dror says, "Some screening is essential to avoid the futures movement from being ruined by dogmatists, self-appointed prophets and well-wishing bearded ignorants."

In a worldwide study of futures research McHale and McHale (1976) offer a classification system based on the activities of the practitioners: forecasters, planners, and futurists. The forecasters go about their work by assuming there are definable causal relations between events through which one can predict their future states as indicated by probability estimates of occurrence. Common examples are technological and economic forecasts. The planners concentrate on plans for the next five to ten years and such efforts are usually applied to a particular sector or segment of society. The values of the planners are implicit in their work, such as raising reading scores based on a national examination. Little attention is given to why these values should be planned. Finally, the futurists concentrate on a time period of ten to 100 years and are explicit about what future is desirable. Much effort is spent on uncovering what actions or policies must be altered if that future is to be realized.

Another way of classifying futures research is offered by McHale based on methodological approaches: descriptive, exploratory, and prescriptive. The descriptive group is less "scientific" and will use such methods as conjecture, speculation, and utopian imagination to describe a desirable future.

The exploratory group tends to base its efforts on methodical extrapolation of past and present conditions to make statements about future states. Economic and technological forecasts, historical records and trends are used to develop a data base for futures projections.

The prescriptive group spends its energies on suggesting futures it deems desirable and prescribes various options, alternatives, and policies for obtaining them. Scenarios, simulations, and gaming theory are often used to "play out" the alternatives.

Debates over what the study of the future should be called may offer a final classification scheme as well as give the reader additional information for studying the field.

An admitted difficulty—but one that underscores the energy, thought, imagination, and freshness of the concept—is that the field does not have a generally accepted name. Futures research, future studies, futuristics, futurism, futuribles, and futurology are all terms used to describe this intellectual effort. The different terms reflect more than just linguistic differences, suggesting that the study of the future is a science, an art, and perhaps even a philosophy.

In 1975 the World Future Society, seeking clarity on the debate, asked its members for their preferred term. Of all the terms only two, future studies and futures research, were judged more positive than negative. Of those polled, 29 percent favored future studies and 25 percent preferred futures research.

Futurology was rejected by 44 percent because to them the term suggests the future can be known scientifically. Their position is best summarized by the French futurist De Jouvenel in his The Art of Conjecture (1967):

> The forecaster who takes care to give his best opinion does not want to make others believe that there is a "science of the future" able to set forth with assurance what will be. He is apprehensive of letting this misunderstanding arise. And it is to prevent this illusion that I reject the term futurology. This word would be very convenient for designating the whole of our forecasting activities except that it would suggest that the results of these activities are scientific—which they are not.

Those who prefer the term future studies argue that it is broad in its meaning and better able to fit many of the field's activities under its label. They prefer it to futures research because to them this term limits the field to scholarly or scientific research. To them, future studies could include scholarly or scientific research, but it could also include artistic and philosophical notions about the future along with attempts to actually create the future environments.

It is difficult to tell if this group actually advocates future studies or really fears futures research and its connotations. In the futures community there are many who fear that the study of the future will be taken over by specialists in think-tanks and universities, or that the field will be dominated by scientific experts.

That there is no general agreement on what the field should be called is reflected by the terms used by major futures writers: Herman Kahn, futurology; Alvin Toffler, futurism; Bertrand de Jouvenel, futuribles; John McHale, future studies; Billy Rojas, futuristics; Dennis Gabor, futuristic studies; Daniel Bell, futurist studies; and Harold Shane, futures research.

In this debate the issues have to be divided and it is clear that the arguments run much deeper than the use of terms. The fight over the terms actually reveals differing viewpoints as to what the field should be doing. There are those who believe the field should be quite active in creating desirable futures, and there are those who feel the area should content itself with exploring and acquiring probable knowledge of what the future will look like. In short, activists versus scholars. Finally there is another group, to which I belong, that argues that the field should include methods for improving policy decisions. The goal of the futures discipline is to aid policy makers so that they will decide wisely among the various courses of action that are always open to those in power. For this philosophical bias, I prefer the term futures research to describe the field. To me this term has a connotation of legitimacy and seriousness that none of the others do. Obviously to me if this new discipline is going to advance, and I mean by that to have impact on policy makers, it will have to do it on the strength of its correctness in its predictions. Because it is a new term seeking to be heard and understood, it must shed any connotations of utopian dream castles and be perceived as a body of knowledge that is useful. Sooner or later in government or industry the futurist will be asked piercing, pragmatic questions like: "What is going to happen?" "What are my options?" "Where is your evidence for this prediction?" After a conference on Friday, these are what I call "Monday morning questions."

Answers to these questions are difficult to come by. But if they are to come at all, it will be through rigorous and systematic methodology. There are some powerful methods in scenario construction —the Delphi technique and cross-impact analysis—for doing futures research. The unique need for the study of the future at the moment is to attract more scholars. As Dror (1973) has concluded, "careful perusal of futures studies literature . . . leads me regretfully but unavoidably to the conclusion that the rate of innovation in futures studies, both in methodology and in substantive ideas, is on a marginally decreasing curve."

If the field is going to be made attractive in the academic community, the best term for this persuasive effort is futures research. If a faculty member is going to explain his annual activities to his dean, he must describe his work in two principal categories, teaching and research.

Finally I have one objection to "future studies" from a communication perspective. To me, this term is potentially confusing because it could be interpreted to mean studies to be made in the future rather than studies of the future. I have a fear that a detailed, highly important study of some future conditions labeled Future Studies could gather dust on a paper-covered policy-maker's desk because he thinks it is a paper on studies to be done in the future. I have spent enough time in state and federal bureaucracies to know that such things do happen.

FUTURES RESEARCH WORLDWIDE

As noted earlier, there has been a shift in futures research from forecasting to exploring and prescribing how particular futures could be achieved.

Between March 1974 and March 1975, McHale and McHale (1976) conducted an international survey of futures research cosponsored with UNITAR (United Nations Institute for Training and Research). The findings of this important work are quite relevant to our discussion and the more salient points will be summarized.

During the past decade the study of the future has undergone some dramatic changes. The shift in research philosophy now seems to indicate that the majority of those conducting work in the field are concerned with "alerting" functions that spell out options and positive and negative consequences from different courses of action. The philosophy of science of the field seems to have moved from prediction to normative goals.

This philosophical movement is also reflected in the change in the number and educational backgrounds of those now coming into the field. In the past five years, futures research has seen an influx of social and behavioral scientists and some scholars from the humanities. This growth is in contrast to the early years when professionals from the physical sciences, engineering, and mathematics dominated the area.

The McHales also note another tendency in that futures research is moving from a kind of "disciplinary enclave towards becoming a social movement." The common or overlapping interest between the ecology and the future(s) seems to be a typical interaction. They also note a third tendency with a growing number of futures secretariats, commissions, or study groups at the national government level.

These trends are summarized by the McHales with a rather clear example. They argue that the field has moved from a pyramid to an hourglass formation. Today there is a large popular base, with a smaller number of scholars in the middle, and a growing number of officials and their organizations (government and industry) at the top.

I In many countries the national government is involved in the study of the future through its planning efforts. This is usually seen in such nations as the USSR, Czechoslovakia, and Poland with five-, ten-, and 25-year plans. Of course the emphasis here is on economics with their centrally planned economies, but there are signs of interest in the future in other noneconomic sectors. For example, in Poland there is research into the future of culture and related methodological problems conducted by the Social Prognoses section at the Institute of Philosophy and Sociology at the Polish Academy of Sciences.

In Sweden Alva Myrdal, former minister of state, was appointed in 1971 to be chairman of a study group chartered to study the future. From this has evolved the Swedish Secretariat for Futures Studies, which is administratively attached to the cabinet office. Their first report, To Choose a Future, published in 1972, discusses future states for Sweden and related policies.

In Denmark the Social Science Research Council set up a Committee for Futurology in 1970. The committee's 1973 report, "Society and Future," surveyed futures work in Denmark and discussed government planning from 1970 through 1985.

In France the government's interest in the study of the future is housed in its Commissariat du Plan, which is concerned with long-range planning. De Jouvenel is in France with his Futuribles group and their related journal, Futuribles: Analyse—Prévision—Prospective. There are a number of important French studies dealing with the future and planning that anyone seriously interested in the field should examine.

In West Germany there is the Ministry of Research and Technology. This official agency's main duty is to define policy options in the technology area.

In the United Kingdom there is the government's Central Policy Review Staff,concerned with national planning. However, much of this nation's futures work has been done by the Social Science Research Council and its Social Forecasting Committee. The Science Policy Research Unit at the University of Sussex has become one of the more important centers of futures research. Also in the United Kingdom the Post Office has been involved in a number of long-range forecasting studies.

In Canada the Special Committee on Science Policy has been involved in futures research on an official basis, and there are a number of nongovernmental futures centers.

FUTURES RESEARCH IN THE UNITED STATES

The United States is a curious contrast to the other nations in terms of an official governmental agency charged with conducting futures research. That this may be coming may have been indicated in 1974 with the introduction of the "foresight" provision in the House Rules in Congress. Although this should not be construed to mean that the House was ordering futures research, it did call for its committees to consider future consequences of legislative and administrative action. Also the Congressional Research Service of the Library of Congress now has a group concerned with providing futures-type information. And the Office of Technology Assessment serves as something of an early warning system as to the impact of technology on society.

The bulk of the futures research done in the United States is done by nongovernmental organizations. The best known are the Rand Corporation in Santa Monica, California, the Hudson Institute in New York, and the Institute for the Future in Menlo Park, California. Many of the current futures methodologies were invented and refined at these institutions.

Another think-tank, Battelle, has conducted the DEMATEL project (DEcision-MAking Trial and Evaluation Laboratory), which is concerned with simulating global policies for dealing with worldwide problems.

In the United States one of the main contributions to futures research was conducted by Daniel Bell who chaired the Commission on the Year 2000 chartered by the American Academy of Arts and Sciences. The 1967 report stimulated public and scholarly interest in the field and serves as a model of how to conduct this type of activity.

In a capitalistic society one cannot ignore the private sector and in the United States business organizations have been engaged in futures research via planning. Four big companies—Du Pont, Scott Paper, Lever Bros., and Monsanto—have been heavily involved in corporate planning for years. About one-third of the financial support for the Institute for the Future comes from private industry. The Delphi technique, discussed in Chapter 8, seems to be the principal methodology used by the Institute and industry for forecasting the future.

Other futures efforts in the United States have involved large numbers of citizens such as the "Hawaii 2000" and "Iowa 2000" projects. Other projects include state and regional groups.

A considerable amount of futures research conducted in the United States is done in academia. The world's first futures research professor, Olaf Helmer, holds the Quinton chair for futures research at the University of Southern California. Helmer, coinventor of the Delphi technique and instrumental in the development of cross-impact analysis, was the second president of the Institute for the Future. Before this he was a senior mathematician at the Rand Corporation.

At the Center for Futures Research, where Helmer is now housed, the emphasis mirrors the research activities in the United States. The center is staffed by university professors and much of the work is conducted for private industry and the State of California. A current project involves work aimed at developing an environmental forecasting tool for corporate planners.

The Stanford Research Institute has created the Social Policy Research Center as the nucleus of futures studies assisting policy makers in the governmental and private sectors to formulate better and higher-quality policies. The Stanford group is concerned with three basic functions: long-range trend analysis and forecasting of alternative futures for the United States; assisting in the formulation of policies in government, business, and quasi-political institutions; and helping to catalyze institutional and social inventions that can help the United States achieve desirable futures.

INTERNATIONAL SOCIETIES AND PROJECTS

Much future-oriented work is done by international societies and related projects. Perhaps the best known group is the Club of Rome and its best-known project, The Limits to Growth. UNESCO has conducted a study dealing with the future of education, and the World Law Fund has finished a project that explores alternative models for future world orders in the next 25 years.

Throughout the world there are a number of societies devoted to studying the future. One of the first, originating in London, is Mankind 2000 and it is important because it provided an early stimulus for futures research. The largest society is the U.S.-based World Future Society, with chapters in several countries. It began with 200 members in 1967 but today has over 12,000 members. It has its own well-known journal, The Futurist, and in 1975 began its own book series with Joseph Martino's An Introduction to Technological Forecasting. Recently the society began to offer a service to help its members find future-related jobs.

Finally there is the World Futures Studies Federation concerned with linking and exchanging information between futures research centers and individuals working in the area on a worldwide basis. In addition, it does carry out conferences and workshops and serves as something of a international liaison structure for people in the field.

EDUCATION IN FUTURES STUDIES

The study of the future is gaining in popularity on U.S. campuses. A survey by Eldredge (1975) reveals that futures education courses are increasing, although many labels are used to describe such courses, ranging from technological forecasting to utopian literature and science fiction.

Despite the growth, Eldredge concludes from his survey that "the badly needed sophisticated research in futures methodology is not developing in university teaching—with possible exceptions in policy studies, technological forecasting and modeling—but rather in public and private think tanks and a few university-affiliated research centers."

California, Wisconsin, and Massachusetts have attempted to futurize educational planning and curricula at both secondary and college levels.

In looking at the methodologies for conducting futures research, the traditional ones are still taught: Delphi, scenario design, cross-impact analysis, and trend extrapolation.

Eldredge's survey reveals that certain disciplines are more involved in teaching futures courses and he offers some tentative explanations for this:

Anthropology. Few in the field have actually taught futures courses, but there have been futures sessions at national meetings seeming to indicate a growing interest in the area.

Business administration. A strong and growing interest here with courses oriented toward technological and market forecasting and a firm conviction that large organizations must plan for the future.

Computer sciences. The interest here is centered in computer simulation courses stressing modeling and systems dynamics.

Economics. Not as much interest here as one would think. Perhaps this stems from a poor record of predicting even short-run business cycles so that there is even greater hesitancy to try to predict the long run. The emphasis has been on quantitative techniques, or as economist E. F. Schumacher is supposed to have said about his colleagues, "They spend their time optimizing the arrangement of the deck chairs on the Titanic."

Education. A lively interest here that is concerned with developing alternative education programs and teaching methods.

Engineering. The emphasis is on courses dealing with technological forecasting and subsequent effects on society.

History. Limited interest with the exceptions of Robert Heilbroner and Frank Manuel.

Sociology. A growing interest and awareness of the relevance of the area to this discipline.

Natural sciences. Issues of energy and ecology seem to have stimulated a new interest in the future.

Several conclusions can be reached from the Eldredge survey. Future studies courses are growing with an estimated growth rate of 50 percent every two years. Some degree programs are now being offered. A graduate program leading to a master's degree in future studies is now offered by the University of Houston. Rather than traditional academic departments, the University of Houston at Clear Lake City is organized around program areas such as individual and social behavior, multicultural studies, resource utilization, and studies of the future. The master's program has some 25 courses, including forecasting techniques, sociology of the future, communications and social change, educational futurism, public policy, business forecasting, and technology assessment. I think the range of the course offerings is in keeping with the need to understand that there are many ways of probing the future.

It seems very important for our educational institutions to begin to offer courses in futures research. Today it is no longer adequate for students to learn only about the past. As Future Shock should have taught us, our current problems are so complex that increasingly we have little lead time for their solutions. A student's psychological survival may depend on courses that allow him to think about the future and what he can do to create desirable futures.

Most students were surprised by race riots, pollution, and lack of energy and increased violence. If our courses had been futures oriented rather than relying on a rearview mirror of the past, it might have come as a surprise but no shock that these problems were coming. In other words, our educational institutions could be using current course offerings to anticipate possible future problems and to teach students to think in an anticipatory way about future consequences.

Glenn (1973) offers a model that could be incorporated into any existing course for dealing with its futures aspects. The learning model can be divided into four sections: (1) in this step each student identifies for himself the trends of the subject for study; (2) each student makes projections to a future date of the impacts on society of these trends; (3) if that future impact is not desirable, each student then describes what would be desirable futures; and (4) each student then works backward in time from the desirable future model to the present in order to grasp what is necessary for that future to occur.

Step 4 is vividly illustrated by Glenn in this example. Think of one leaf on a tree as a desirable future model among many other leaves (other futures). For the water to get from the roots to the leaf, it has to follow many "forks" in the road. These forks may be viewed as decision or action points as in a PERT or DELTA chart. The water has to make the right decision at each fork or the leaf will die. Similarly, certain actions or policies must be made for the desirable future to grow out of the present. Thus the students have the learning experience of figuring out what steps are necessary in order to reach their desirable future.

FUTURES RESEARCH AND SCIENCE

A final issue—futures research scientific—needs to be dealt with here. This question is an interesting one because the academics are afraid it is not, while the activists are fearful that it is. Both fears are based on misconceptions of what science is.

The issue of "science" was discussed in more detail in the first three chapters so it will be discussed only in summary fashion here.

De Jouvenel has argued that there cannot be any science of the future and prefers to describe futures research methodology as the "art of conjecture."

I would argue that futures research can use the scientific method to make better predictions. Because of the pragmatic nature of futures research, the discipline or field is always going to be asked to make more predictions than explanations. The intellectual worth of the field will ultimately be judged on the quality of the decisions it produces rather than on its hindsight or explanatory power. The urgency of our problems like energy, crime, and mental health does not allow the time for building traditional scientific theory. Instead, the futures researcher is asked for his advice today—tomorrow is too late.

Given that the futures researcher is going to have no choice but to be concerned with predictions, the best methodological tools for doing this must be gathered. It is important to pause for a moment and recall that science has normally advanced from description to explanation to prediction and that futures research is only following tradition.

In Chapter 1 I argued that methodology needs to be considered as a philosophical point of departure. That methodology is much more than mere techniques. Keeping this in mind, it is helpful to remember that the "scientific method" is as much philosophy as it is technique. The scientific method depends on empirical observation rather than dogma for its body of knowledge. It seems to me that this is exactly what futures research is doing. It observes events (empirical data) from the past and the present to make predictions about the future.

These forecasts are not scientific predictions in the traditional view of science in which predictions are based on theory and natural laws. The field is too new for much theoretical knowledge to have accumulated, and the questions beg for immediate answers. The futures researcher realizes this and simply proceeds as best he can, knowing that his models or predictions can be improved with more experience and data. In other words, many of his predictions are of course conditional. It tells what future(s) will occur if particular initial conditions and events hold. But certainly the conditional quality applies to any scientific prediction. For example, in chemistry various laws are postulated on the initial conditions of standard temperature and pressure. An inert gas can be predicted to behave in a certain way only if certain initial conditions are met.

In traditional science (that based on mechanics) the hypothetical-deductive technique of testing hypotheses is substituted for the scientific method. This is an unfortunate intellectual path because many of our large complex social problems cannot be meaningfully tested using hypotheses. One cannot control nor manipulate crime in a U.S. city as one might a test tube of chemical solution. Thus the difficult problem of how to perform social experiments on future time periods is difficult enough without being handicapped by the wrong intellectual approach.

Traditional science as in physics has always dealt with a closed mechanical or nonliving system. But in 1977 we are beginning to learn that even what we thought were closed systems may in fact be open (subject to external controls and conditions). Thus our models for predicting the future must move beyond this traditional science concept of closed or mechanistic systems and on to ones that are open systems or living constructs.

It would seem that history would be an important concept for constructing such models. If one applies General Systems Theory to history, then history can be seen as an open system in the sense that had this or that occurred the course of history would have changed. This permits us to view history as something other than a closed system following an inevitable path. History then becomes an important intellectual fulcrum for the futures researcher because it may teach him where the crucial initial conditions and decision points are for controlling the future. The basic method used by Kahn and Wiener (1967) was to identify long-term trends that would seem likely to continue. Using a historical framework one spots a trend and extrapolates it into the future. The difficulty is of course in the assumption that the trend will continue, and this in turn likely depends on various conditions. The futures researcher must be careful not to forget the dependence of trends on initial conditions. If he does he will likely engage in prophecy rather than scientific prediction.

Finally I would argue that futures research is scientific in that, like traditional science, it does seek to build up theory. Remember that the etymological origin of "theory" is the Greek theoros, that is, "a spectator." Different spectators have different perceptions of the progress of the game. For one group the umpire clearly called the ball a strike while another group saw it as just the opposite. And so it is with theory. A theory can be a way of looking at phenomena, neither correct nor incorrect, but simply from different perspectives. Theory construction can perform an important task in the research effort—bringing a heuristic quality to the effort. Heuristic used as an adjective means "serving to discover." This is consistent with futures research that is seeking to discover alternative futures. Once a theory has enough concepts, terms, and rules of syntax to make prediction possible (based on conditions and probabilities), it can be elevated to the rank of "discipline."

I believe futures research, having followed the scientific method, is now ready for this status. Through prediction, futures research enables the policy maker to make informed choices. Or as Ashby (1964) notes: "The sailor who knows that there will be a storm can change his course or seek a harbor. We say . . . that the organism has reacted to the threat rather than to the disaster itself, and has thus forestalled the disaster." An objective worthy of science.

REFERENCES

Amara, Roy. 1975. "Some Observations on the Interaction of Technology and Society." Futures, December.

Ashby, W. R. 1964. An Introduction to Cybernetics. London: Methuen.

Beer, Stafford. 1975. Platform for Change. New York: Wiley.

Dror, Yehezkel. 1973. "A Third Look at Futures Studies." Technological Forecasting and Social Change 5.

de Jouvenel, Bertrand. 1967. The Art of Conjecture. New York: Basic Books.

Eldredge, H. 1975. "University Education in Futures Studies." The Futurist, April.

Emery F., and E. Trist. 1965. "The Causal Texture of Organizational Environments." Human Relations 18, no. 1.

Gabor, Dennis. 1964. Inventing the Future. New York: Knopf.

Glenn, J. 1973. "Forecasting Techniques as Teaching Methods." Technological Forecasting and Social Change 5.

Kahn, Herman, and Anthony Wiener. 1967. The Year 2000. New York: Macmillan.

McHale, J., and M. C. McHale. 1976. "An Assessment of Futures Studies Worldwide." Futures, April.

Priban, I. 1975. "A Framework for the Future." Futures, April.

Toffler, Alvin. 1970. Future Shock. New York: Random House.

_____. 1972. The Futurists. New York: Random House.

6
Objectives Trees

Since World War II, energy usage has been a classic Malthusian case of exponential growth, so that in the 1950s and 1960s the world has consumed more than had been used up in all previous human history. Oil production should peak out around the world in the early 1990s. The world, which is now consuming about 60 million barrels a day, faces a limit on production somewhere around 75 million or 80 million barrels a day. That means in five years' time we will have used up most of the possibility of further expansion of oil production.

As energy continues to decline, one may ask what we can do to prevent a doomsday crisis now. Now? Almost nothing. If we had started planning for the energy crisis 20 years ago, we would have had more time to plan and cope. If we had started 50 years ago, it would have been easy.

The current energy crisis is a classic case of a lack of planning, resulting in a lack of lead time to cope with the problem. Gaining lead time through planning can mean the difference between skittering off the cliff in a blind way or stopping at the edge.

PLANNING

What is planning? Planning is anticipatory decision making. Planning is a thinking process in which a system selects courses of action and outcomes for situations that have not yet occurred but are expected to occur in the near future. This definition stress the close relationship between planning and the decision-making process, and it is future oriented because the system makes a choice now as to how it would like its state or condition to be in the future.

This does not mean the planning is easy. The energy crisis or any other dozen problems tell us that. To say to an administrator or policy maker, "Plan now!" is to expect him to be a good thinker, teacher, and policy maker at the same time. This is very difficult, and for the same kind of reasons a physician does not as a rule practice medicine on himself. Thus a policy maker needs to get outside help. A form of help is available from social scientists and particular methodologies suitable for planning efforts. This chapter will discuss planning only briefly and then will take up in detail a planning methodology, objectives trees.

The solution of real problems—those problems that affect our lives directly, like energy—provides a unique opportunity for policy makers and social scientists to learn from one another.

The social scientist has much to learn from the pragmatic realities confronting the policy maker, and the policy maker has much to learn from the theoretical world of the social scientist. This is not to say that one is more realistic than the other, as they are both working on the same problem but from different perspectives. The point is that each is dependent on the other and neither can wait until the other is finished before beginning his own task.

Planning is an effort to spot or anticipate problems; it looks toward the future to give meaning and feasibility to current choices, and the close relationship between planning and decision making is evident. A decision maker is faced with selecting outcomes or choices of action in a particular situation. Planning involves the same behaviors, but these are related to future choice situations.

Ackoff (1971) has suggested three temporal attitudes toward the future relevant to planning. These are the reactive attitude, which suggests a policy of wait and see; the preactive attitude, which involves predicting the future and preparing for it; and the interactive attitude, which attempts to design a future and make it happen. The first time frame, reactive, implies that the system is crisis-management oriented. It does not try to anticipate future problems and subsequent actions, but simply deals with them as they arise. It concentrates on short-term objectives. The preactive temporal attitude implies the system anticipates future situations and choices. The interactive implies that the system not only anticipates the future and related choices, but also that it attempts to design and affect the future situations.

In summary, planning attempts to make decision making better; not easier, but always better decisions. It does this by making choices or options more plentiful and their related consequences more obvious. In a sense, it makes decisions more rational. The rational basis comes from a rigorous analysis of alternative actions (choices) based on empirical data generated by scientific methodology, tempered by the pragmatism of the real world.

Certainly this is not an easy task. Only the naive would think so. The complexity of the planning task suggests that such an undertaking would require many minds of expertise to contribute to it. That is, planning is best utilized as a group project with various people bringing ideas and knowledge to the exercise. This is why the early part of the chapter suggested that the social scientist and policy maker could learn from each other when engaged in planning. The policy maker is concerned with prediction—what is going to happen and what will happen if I do this—and so is the social scientist. He too in his science has followed a path of description, explanation, and ultimately prediction. Both are concerned with prediction and increasing the reliability of those predictions.

Jantsch (1969) has offered an idealized process of planning involving four activities: forecasting, planning, decision making, and rational creative action. These activities take place at three levels: the operational or tactical, the strategic, and the policy level. Using these ideas, Jantsch offers three levels or time dimensions to planning: efforts to deal with present activities, those dealing with the feasibility of new activities, and those dealing with alternative future activities. Such a time frame could be even more related to planning methodology as in the case of meeting planning goals and objectives. In general, goals are idealized states that the system always aspires to reach, such as "improve the outputs"or"improve patient care." There is always room for improvement so the system is always attempting to meet its idealized goals. Objectives are obtainable. They can be reached and measurement is possible so that a system may know when it has met its objectives, such as "to learn French this semester as demonstrated by passing an exam." Long-term planning has to do with those activities related to goals, while middle- or short-term planning are concerned with meeting objectives. This chapter is concerned with planning activities related to achieving objectives. Hence, the methodology will be "objectives trees."

PLANNING AND COMMUNICATING

Linstone (1969) has noted four major difficulties in long-range planning:

Long-range objectives are frequently unsuitable for needs analysis.
The "system" is inadequately understood.
There is a poor meshing of objectives, environment, and needs.
Acceptance of new needs poses overwhelming sociological, psychological, legal, or organizational difficulties. Organizational inflexibility and short-term orientation stand in the way of the acceptance of major innovations.

For any organization, the selection of policy options is going to require good effective communication between various levels of participants. The interpersonal relationships will play a major part of the total planning process. However, we can conclude if the policy options generated through careful planning are effectively communicated to others the acceptance of the selected options will be easier. Clearly, communication plays a crucial role if planning methodology is to be implemented. The problems of the difficulty of communicating are compounded when one recalls the complexity of the problem to be dealt with. Planning, by its nature, attempts to cope with complex problems that are ill-defined and usually inadequately understood. Identifying the most responsive communication channels is necessary if policy makers and social scientists are to assist one another. Thus the concept of planning involves two levels: identifying and selecting policy options, and communicating such decisions to those who must understand and implement the selected choices.

I propose a conceptual model of the planning process that lays out five explicit roles: describe and set the parameters of the problem; identify policy options; state the system's goals and objectives; communicate the selected options to all those involved; and evaluate the attainment of the goals and objectives.

Related to the communication difficulties inherent in the planning process is the real-world observation that many administrators or policy makers do not plan, or if they do they do not follow the plans in their daily decision-making activities. This is unfortunate because it has been my experience that future events with high probabilities of occurrence—which are easily detected—usually have small to modest impacts upon the system while those with low probabilities of occurrence—which are difficult to detect—usually have large to catastrophic impacts upon the system. Clearly some improved system of surveillance or planning is needed to spot problems and develop coping strategies. In short, some form of surveillance radar is needed for today's complexity. It is suggested here that objectives trees could function in this way.

WHAT ARE OBJECTIVES TREES?

From a communication perspective, what is really needed is some methodological device that can clearly identify policy options. As called for in Chapter 3, a simple graphic communication tool, an objectives tree, can provide the gestalt for dealing with complexity.

One begins an objectives tree with the most important objective stated at the top of the tree with lesser objectives written below. In other words, an objectives tree is a hierarchy of objectives. It is constructed in graph form with circles, squares, or rectangles (the user's choice) representing the objectives, and the relationships between them are illustrated by connecting lines. This is shown in Figure 6.1.

FIGURE 6.1
An Objectives Tree

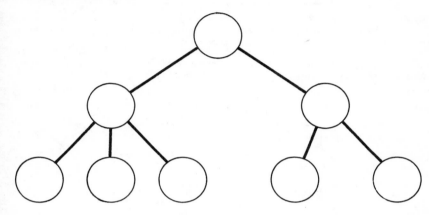

Source: Compiled by the author.

Figure 6.1 illustrates the conceptual idea of an objectives tree. Objectives, according to Warfield (1971), are defined as a set of verbs in the infinitive form (action words) and a set of objective phrases (words upon which the action takes place). Using this definition the policy maker can develop specific objectives and define the relationships between them. This can also be illustrated in graph form as in Figure 6.2.

Figure 6.2 is representative of the basic requirements of an objectives tree. The top or prime objective, "To devise and implement a comprehensive national energy policy," is located at the top of the tree, or level 1. Level 2 is composed of second-order objectives: "To do nothing," "To develop new technology," and "to conserve energy." Finally we find a third level of objectives: "To increase coal production," "To use solar energy," and "To use nuclear power," all subobjectives to meet the level 2 objective, "To develop new technology." Obviously the tree is hierarchical.

While an objectives tree is constructed to produce pragmatic policy options, it can be used to develop theoretical statements as

FIGURE 6.2

An Objectives Tree with Objectives at Three Levels

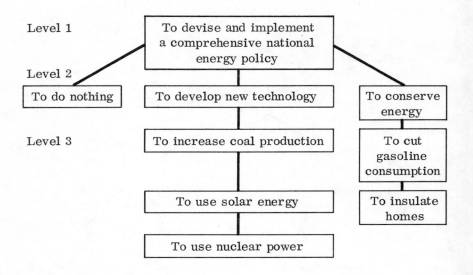

Source: Compiled by the author.

well. That is, an objectives tree can be constructed from any level of abstraction. In fact, it could begin with a goal and then proceed toprime objectives and subobjectives. This flexibility is consistent with the earlier arguments for General Systems Theory: to be able to attack a complex problem at different levels. For example, the level 3 objective, "To cut gasoline consumption," could be pulled out and made into a prime objective by the policy maker. Subobjectives could then include: "To raise the price per gallon at the pump," "To impose a graduated excise tax on new cars that do not meet federal average mileage standards," "To give a rebate to those who buy small, more economical cars." Of course, each of these could have subobjectives. The point here is to show that a policy maker can construct an objectives tree to suit his needs.

CONSTRUCTING AN OBJECTIVES TREE

To begin the construction of an objectives tree, one must have a set of objectives. This set may exist in the form of previous objectives or one may have to generate objectives from scratch. If you have to generate objectives, follow a procedure similar to "brainstorming" in managerial circles. Simply write down all the objectives you or others can think of without regard to priorities, levels, or quality. The time for analysis is later, not now. The important first step is to generate some objectives.

Next write the objectives on 3" by 5" cards and stick them to a cork board. This gives an overall view of the stated objectives—in a sense, a graphic gestalt. Now comes what I refer to as geometry of the mind. This means arranging and rearranging the objectives until they fall into some form of order or logic for you. This is where the objectives are arranged in some hierarchial form. Remember the structure of your objectives graph will be similar to what mathematicians formally refer to as a tree structure.

This hierarchial arrangement is accomplished by asking the question "How?" at every level of the tree. In our earlier example the question, "How to devise and implement a comprehensive national energy policy?" was answered, "To develop new technology," and "To conserve energy." The question, "How to conserve energy?" was answered, "To cut gasoline consumption," and "To insulate homes." The question "How?" is simply asked of each objective.

As one reads the answers to the "How" at lower levels, the detail of how each objective is achieved increases. When constructing an objectives tree in this fashion one may find that gaps will appear in the original set of objectives and new objectives will have to be generated to fill them.

An interesting sidelight to this type of construction is to ask the question "Why?" Suppose one is examining some level of subobjectives in a large objectives tree. If the particular subobjective seems odd or unclear in relation to the overall tree, one can uncover the reason for it by asking "Why?" and tracing the connecting line to the next (higher) level objective. By asking "Why?" one can find the reason for the occurrence of a particular objective. The "Why" question does not construct an objectives tree but it may help explain one.

As for the final form of an objectives tree structure, it may be traditionally hierarchical or vertical, or it can be constructed in a horizontal or linear fashion. Either is correct and is simply the choice of the builder. Figures 6.1 and 6.2 were in vertical or hierarchical form. Other examples that follow will be illustrated using the horizontal or linear (read left to right) format. For example, the objectives tree in Figure 6.2 can be illustrated in linear form as in Figure 6.3.

An additional bit of realism or sophistication can be added to the construction of an objectives tree in the form of barriers to meet-

FIGURE 6.3
An Objectives Tree with Objectives at Three Levels
  in Horizontal or Linear Format

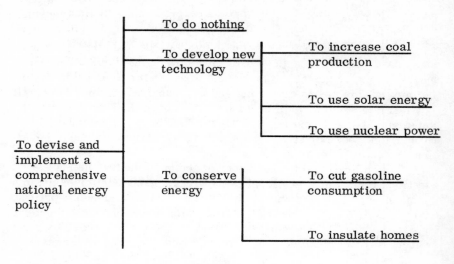

Source: Compiled by the author.

ing the objectives. Essentially objectives are written and then barriers that would hinder or prevent the accomplishment of the objectives are written. We can illustrate this added element to the objectives tree graphically as shown in Figure 6.4.

FIGURE 6.4
Graphic Display of Barriers to Objectives

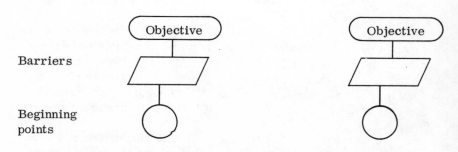

Source: Compiled by the author.

Consider the objective, "To cut gasoline consumption," and the beginning point would be the nationwide announcement of such a policy. However, the careful planner would realistically realize that there would be barriers hindering or stopping the implementation. Such barriers could include a reluctance by people to cut gasoline consumption, or car manufacturers' refusal or inability to build automobiles that consume less gasoline. For the objective to be realized, such barriers would have to be overcome. This may mean the generation of objectives to accomplish this, but the identification of barriers in the planning stage of policy formation is much better than after a task is under way. PPBS failed as a budget system under the Johnson administration because mid-level managers would not implement it; this is an example of a barrier that was not recognized by top administration officials.

If a barrier cannot be overcome even though it has been identified, an objectives tree structure may reveal alternative ways around it as is done with PERT charts. Assume our energy saving objective is "To insulate 90 percent of all American homes," but an immediate barrier is the cost to the homeowner. However, some alternative objectives for overcoming this barrier could include tax credits for home insulation materials; or if homeowners prefer, they may take advantage of a weatherization service offered by utility companies. In this instance, the utilities would pay for the improvements or provide reasonable financing and arrange for the contractors. The customer would pay for the improvements through small, regular additions to monthly utility bills. In most cases these additional charges would be almost entirely offset by lower energy consumption brought about by energy savings. It is estimated that 40 percent of a home's heat escapes because of lack of insulation. In this example, there is a barrier, a homeowner's inability to buy insulation, overcome through additional objective alternatives.

THE SIGNIFICANCE OF OBJECTIVES TREES

As has been noted earlier in previous chapters, social problems are exceedingly complex and the organizations or managerial systems that attempt to solve and cope with them rival their complexity. Anyone who has attempted to get needed information from the U.S. Department of Health, Education and Welfare in Washington, D.C. knows the enormity of his task. Thus when a system is attempting to formulate a policy for handling a complex topic, some gestalt of the work to be done is needed. In fact, some way to structure the problem and the associated policies are needed. This chapter has argued that an objectives tree is such a methodology. Some comprehensive planning design is necessary for success. Such a planning design may have to overcome conceptual barriers because of the sheer complexity of the task. In addition, some measure of progress is needed for the policy maker to be sure he is going in the right direction. A detailed five-year policy needs evaluation points along the way to measure its progress rather than waiting until the end of five years to see if it accomplished its task.

Because evaluations are made along the way, the objectives tree structure can be used to determine if the original policy reflects a workable approach to the problem. One may find that certain objectives formed in the planning stage can be met for various reasons: social, legal, personal, or financial. Thus an objectives tree can be viewed as an element of the policy planning system or an organization.

An objectives tree is useful in that it may allow the planner or policy maker to delegate authority more evenly and clearly. It is doubtful that all objectives have to be worked on at once and with the same level of energy. Some objectives require immediate attention while others can wait. This means that staff personnel do not all have to pursue one objective until it is done; some of them can be shifted as the need arises to other objectives. Talent and energy can be shifted in a very flexible way because many of the objectives are interdependent. Yet the project director does not lose sight of what personnel are doing because progress reports on meeting objectives are fed back to him.

On any complex project people may be added at various time points when their services are needed. This can create a problem of integration as they must "get up to speed," but they may be unclear as to what they are supposed to be doing or what has been accomplished prior to their coming on board. An objectives tree structure can provide them with an overall picture of the project while the detailed sub-objectives can provide them with details for their immediate tasks. If a project employee does not understand why he is being asked to do something, he can ask "Why?" and get an answer by following the line to the higher-level objective. In short, an objectives tree can make the managerial tasks much easier because the "hows and whys" are spelled out.

In addition, by being able to survey the entire project, new personnel may see various objectives that attract them more or that they feel they could help to accomplish. This may help to uncover additional talent and energies for the organization. For example, a person may have been hired as a technical writer, but while looking at the overall objectives trees spots an objective, "To develop questionnaire." Since he has expertise in this area he can offer to help accomplish this objective.

Related to the above discussion, an objectives tree also imposes a strict discipline on all those engaged in the planning effort. The constant asking of "How" and "Why" forces one to concentrate solely on the task at hand. This is extremely important when dealing with a complex problem. That it does this is seen in the generation of barriers, alternatives, levels of objectives, and interdependencies among all elements. In dealing with complexity, it is common for the participants to lose their focus and begin to discuss other points about the problem. The sequential nature of the objectives tree structure forces a rigorous form of thinking.

Along with forcing rigorous thinking on what is to be accomplished, objectives trees tend to force precision in the planners' use of language. The required format for forming an objective phrase leads to precision usually not found in lengthy statements. In a sense, the objective phrases function like operational definitions in the policy-making efforts.

One of the problems with methodology is that there is a tendency to never check the original assumptions. Contemporary history is full of societal failures because original assumptions were never re-examined for validity. Too often methodology is used to correct techniques that failed, rather than questioning the established goal. Vietnam is a tragic example. By requiring a flow of answers to the questions of how and why, objectives trees often lead one back to the original goal or prime objective. It tends to generate the question, "Why are we doing this?" And this may likely lead to the challenging and reformulating of original intent by policy makers.

This suggests that an objectives tree may function as a change agent in a system. The generation of new questions and/or new information may lead to change, and for those convinced of the need for such changes, an objectives tree can provide hard data and logical reasoning.

It seems obvious to conclude from all of the above points concerning an objectives tree that an overwhelming advantage is that it functions as a communication medium. In fact, this may be its single largest advantage. Intrinsically, it reflects the capacity for generating a communication gestalt called for in Chapter 3 and embodied in other methodologies discussed in this book. It provides a picture by which people may communicate and reach a consensus concerning a complex problem. As Licklider and Taylor (1968) note:

> When people communicate face to face they externalize
> their models so that they can be sure they are talking about
> the same thing. Even such a simple externalized model as
> a flow diagram or an outline—because it can be seen by all
> the communicators—serves as a focus for the discussion.
> It changes the nature of communications. When communi-
> cators have no such common framework they merely make

speeches at each other; but when they have a manipulable model before them, they utter a few words, point, sketch, nod or object.

In short, the objectives tree superimposes a common referent or operational definition of the task at hand in the communication flow between all participants.

Too often when dealing with complexity, as in a societal problem, goals and objectives are not made explicit. Such planning elements are discussed in general terms. A policy for action cannot be based on such generalities. Specifics are needed. It has been my experience that this is not done unless a formal tool is used. Serving as this type of formal tool, an objectives tree stimulates creative discussion, generates objectives, and identifies barriers and alternatives. Through its communicative ability an objectives tree provides distinct objectives for specific programs and rather explicit suggestions for overall policy formulation. On the implementation side, it serves management as a stimulus for consensus, because it serves as a map for the territory to be charted.

The intent behind the objectives tree is to stimulate creative generation of policy through objectives arranged in a hierarchical fashion with a clear relationship between them. That it does this, along with being a communication medium via a graphic model, is testimony for using such a procedure when making policy.

REFERENCES

Ackoff, R. 1971. "Principles of Planning," mimeograph. Paper presented at University of Pennsylvania.

Jantsch, E. 1969. "From Forecasting and Planning to Policy Sciences." Paper presented at American Association for the Advancement of Science, Boston, December.

Licklider, J. C. R., and R. Taylor. 1968. "The Computer as a Communications Device." Science and Technology, April.

Linstone, H. 1969. "When Is a Need a Need?" Technological Forecasting 1.

Warfield, J., and J. D. Hill. 1971. "Development of a Unified Systems Engineering Concept." Systems Engineering Workshop Notebook. Seattle: Battelle.

7
The Delta Chart: An Aid to Social Science Research

For the social scientist serving as project director of a large research project, several critical decisions that he has to make involve the planning and monitoring of the research design. As the chief decision maker for the project, he must have a clear concept of what activities and events are necessary within a given length of time. In addition he must identify key decision points for data collection in the research design, allocate resources, and modify the research strategy to fit prevailing circumstances.

Of critical importance to the project director is the need for effective communication between himself and the other persons working on the research study. Since the problem under attack is complex and the project lengthy, it is likely that the study will employ the expertise of many professionals—a team approach with coordinated activities. Although their efforts may be done individually, in the final analysis they are working together as members of the research team. The project director must decide which of these activities must come first, which ones must be finished before another can begin, and which ones may be carried out at the same time. In essence he needs an overview of the set of research activities to be carried out, and he needs to be able to illustrate the interdependency of the individually assigned project activities.

What is sorely needed is a communication device that would clearly and concisely display the research project. Such a device would ideally picture (visually display) an overview of the research project that could be grasped in a few moments of study by each research participant; show the connecting interdependencies between each activity; identify critical decision points; provide appropriate levels of detail; offer feedback loops for altering certain activities if necessary; and finally provide a basis for monitoring and reporting on the progress of the project over time.

This chapter offers such a communication device—a diagrammatic display of these needs—the DELTA chart. A form of flow chart, DELTA is an acronym for the five types of graphic symbols used in the chart: Decision box, Event box, Logic box, Time arrow, and Activity box. These key symbols are shown in Figure 7.1 .

FIGURE 7.1

DELTA Chart Symbols

Source: Compiled by the author.

ELEMENTS OF DELTA CHARTS

The decision box, as indicated by its name, is where the project director must choose between alternatives. Normally three alternatives will be depicted by a decision box. One, based on the successful completion of preceding activities, will be a decision to go on to the next set of activities. A second will suggest that some or all of the preceding activities must be redone before work can begin on the next round of activities. A third, though more drastic, alternative is that the decision is made to stop current activities until correcting strategies are implemented. A decision box with the three common alternatives as would appear in a DELTA chart is shown in Figure 7.2. For identification purposes the decision-maker's title (here, the project director) is written in the decision box.

An event box represents a clear point in time at which something (an event) has happened. Although such an event may result from much previous work, it actually requires no work or time from the project director when following the DELTA chart. For example, an

FIGURE 7.2
Decision Box with Three Alternatives

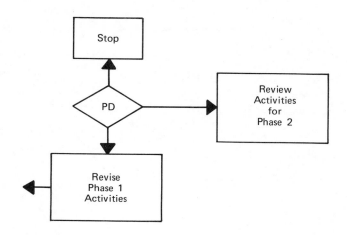

Source: Compiled by the author.

event might be described as "contract awarded from National Institute of Mental Health." Certainly much work preceded the event through the writing of the proposal, and so on, but on the DELTA chart it represents only a beginning point for the project director and does not demand any additional work or time. To help make a clear distinction between "events" and "activities," a syntax is assigned to these DELTA chart elements. An event is written as a noun or object followed by a verb or action phrase such as "contract awarded." On the DELTA chart an event box may be divided into three parts, depending on the level of detail required by the project director. In the upper portion the event is defined. The event is identified in the lower right corner and the event date is written in the lower left. An event box is shown in Figure 7.3.

The logic box represents the logical functions of the event and activity boxes. Two such functions, AND/OR, are currently used in DELTA chart construction. The AND box may appear at the beginning or end of an event or activity box, or may be viewed systemically as inputs or outputs. Should the AND be used as an input (beginning) to an event or activity, then the logic function commands that all the events, activities, or decisions feeding into the AND must occur before any subsequent activities or events can take place. Should an AND function be used as the output (end) of an event or activity, then

FIGURE 7.3

An Event Box

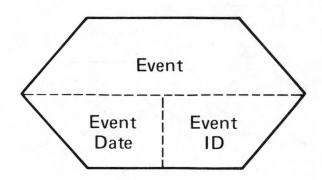

Source: Compiled by the author.

all events, activities, or decisions connected to it must take place. A third use may also be made for the AND function. The outputs of events, activities, or decisions that have occurred may be connected to an AND box and then subsequently be connected to future events, activities, and decisions that will occur. Figure 7.4 illustrates the AND logic box.

The OR logic box when used in a DELTA chart means that only one event, activity, or decision feeding into an OR box can be accomplished at that time. Consequently the OR box has only one output.

Time is shown on a DELTA chart through the time arrow symbol. In DELTA chart construction the lines that connect the various elements (boxes) represent the flow of time, except at the decision box where the outputs or decisions are illustrated by lines. Having the connecting lines represent only time (with the decision box exception) marks the DELTA chart in sharp contrast with other networks for in them lines usually reflect activities that occur over time. A DELTA chart time arrow is shown in Figure 7.5.

The activity element, in contrast with an event as discussed earlier, represents a specific task requiring a known quantity of labor and other resources for it to occur. The syntax of the activity element also contrasts with an event, requiring an active verb followed by an object word or phrase such as "construct questionnaire." On the DELTA chart an activity box may be divided into four parts. The largest portion designates the activity, while the top part of the box names the person or organization responsible for completing the ac-

FIGURE 7.4
AND Logic Boxes

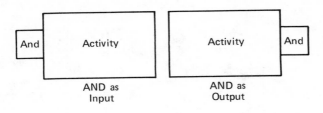

AND as
Input

AND as
Output

AND Logic Boxes

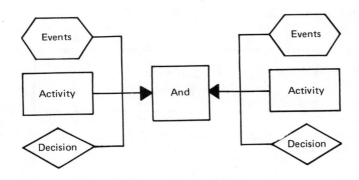

AND as conjunction point

Source: Compiled by the author.

tivity. The activity identification (usually number or letter) is in the lower right corner, while the time needed to complete the activity is placed in the lower left corner of the box. An activity box is shown in Figure 7.6.

CONSTRUCTION OF A DELTA CHART

For the administrator the research plan actually begins with his decision, as project director, to construct a DELTA chart to guide the project. A general procedure for constructing a DELTA chart is

FIGURE 7.5

Time Arrows

Source: Compiled by the author.

FIGURE 7.6

Activity Box

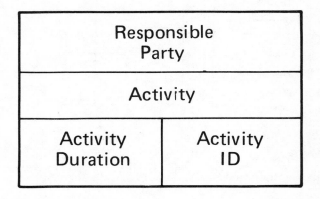

Source: Compiled by the author.

shown in Figure 7.7. The chart depicts three levels of construction complexity. The second and third levels are not mandatory for DELTA chart construction, but they can be used if needed. Normally they are used in only long complex studies. The first level shows only the appropriate elements (boxes), but the second level calls for an identifying code for each symbol, usually a numeral 1.0, 1.2, and so on. The third level requires a time estimate as to how long a particular event, activity, or decision will require before completion. This may be

FIGURE 7.7

How to Construct a DELTA Chart

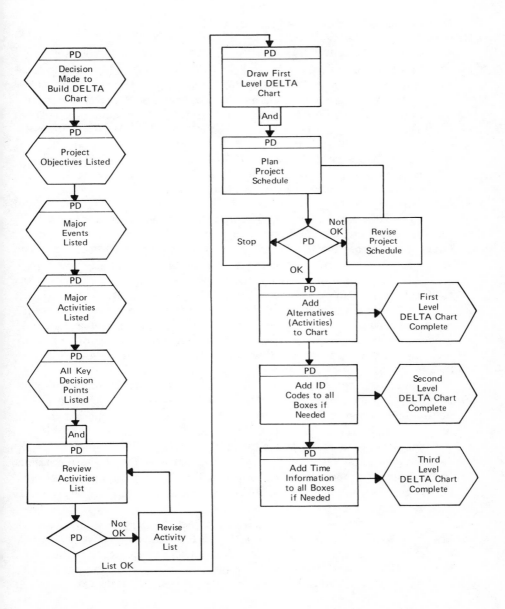

Source: Compiled by the author.

days, weeks, months, and so on. Figure 7.6 illustrates the second and third levels of construction complexity.

DELTA AS A COMMUNICATION DEVICE

As noted earlier, the DELTA chart is a form of flow chart. It was developed in R&D circles as a tool for planning and guiding activities in a research project. Such efforts can be done to some extent by other network methods such as PERT (Program Evaluation Review Technique) but these do not offer the flexibility often needed in R&D projects. It is argued here that typical communication research projects require the flexibility of a DELTA chart.

Too often a crucial concept is left out of the research plan for the project—interpersonal communication. The DELTA chart can become the tool for achieving this communication through its diagrammatic display of the project's activities.

The flow chart diagram represents the single best overview of the research project. In essence it communicates that based on our current estimates the future progress of the project will occur as shown in the diagram. It functions as a model, graphically providing an intelligible, visual picture of the objectives to be met, activities to be done, and the interdependency of all project elements.

A complex project research requires too much energy, money, and time to waste. Yet all research planning requires human judgment, and waste can occur if someone (usually the project director) must assume work is proceeding according to the plan only to find that it is not.

The logic and control of the DELTA chart is much more comprehensible than the same material written out in prose. Without an easily understood physical picture of the whole project, errors in judgment will often occur. The discipline of the DELTA chart's logic will help to avoid errors in the overall planning of the project. The various people involved in the research may tend to view their particular activities as separated and isolated, but they are actually part of an integrated whole. This capability is especially helpful when several organizations or consultants are involved in the project, because they can see how they must work together to meet the project's objectives. The DELTA chart leaves little doubt to all those concerned that they are an important part of the whole plan. The communicative ability of the DELTA chart also makes it a particularly good medium for presenting an easily understood project picture that is easily grasped by a wide audience.

Since the DELTA chart is a flow chart it can offer more flexibility in research planning than networks (like PERT, CPM, and so on) because flow charts can display conditional activities depending on predecessor activity outcomes. This advantage of increased flexibility more closely parallels the real research environment than do the restraints of traditional networks. For example a CPM (Critical Path Method) network diagram represents only one plan for achieving a goal. However, in the world of social research, experimental results cannot be known beforehand. The dangers of following only one research plan through a priori elimination of project options have been noted by Sipper (1970).

The DELTA chart does attempt to list alternative research activities and does communicate the important research restraint that the project's direction and progress is determined by the outcome of preceding activities. The feedback concept is also utilized by the DELTA chart. As can be seen in Figure 7.7 a "yes" answer at the decision point (the diamond-shaped box) means that previous activities have successfully been completed. But a "no" answer loops back to where additional study or experimentation may be necessary or an activity must be repeated. Each decision point contains one feedback loop for repeating or revising previous activities. This feedback loop reflects the DELTA chart's superior flexibility over network methods and more realistically reflects the uncertainty in communication research outcomes. The only certainty in most long, complex research projects is that the original research plan will have to be changed. Activities and time estimates usually have to be modified to some extent to deal with the changes imposed by the real world such as variables in the research environment, decreasing resources, peculiarities of the data, and so on.

DELTA AS A PLANNING AND MONITORING INSTRUMENT

In the planning of a research project by the project director, what are needed are systematic, logical methods for organizing the communication research. This is no easy task, as Holloman (1965) has noted that the management of research is a science in itself.

PERT, as the name would imply, was originally developed to review and evaluate completed research projects for the navy. Although PERT can be used as a planning instrument, its origins bias it toward after-the-fact evaluations. DELTA, with its emphasis on future activities, is thus superior to PERT for planning a research project. In addition the vocabulary of PERT is more limited than that of DELTA, lacking decision and logic elements. This limitation of PERT may restrict planning, resulting in a tendency to plan for only one approach to the research project. PERT's lack of clearly defined decision points makes it difficult for the project director to identify who is responsible for the various activities.

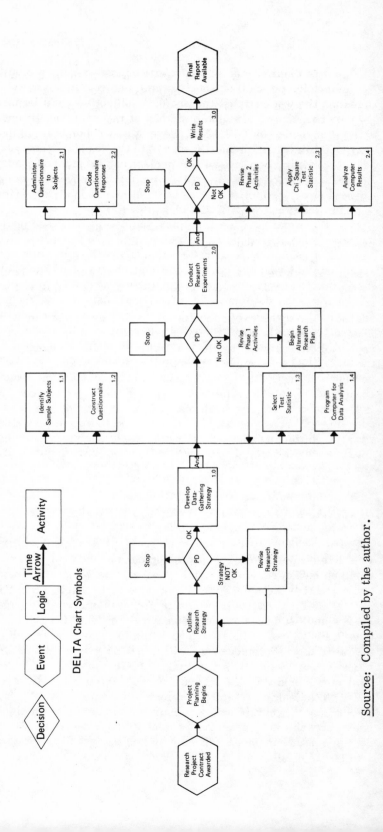

FIGURE 7.8

Abbreviated DELTA Chart for Hypothetical Research Project

Source: Compiled by the author.

It is clear that a DELTA chart can be used as a monitoring instrument for controlling the research project; in other words, controlling the work so that the project's objectives will be met. As the work progresses, a reliable method of reporting occurrences of activities is provided by DELTA. These status reports are important and provide almost immediate feedback to the project director.

Additional control of the project can be gained by adapting other network techniques to the DELTA chart. Specifically, computer programs developed for PERT to calculate time and cost estimates are equally applicable to DELTA charts.

For small and less complex projects, additional project control can be gained through the DELTA chart by relating it to the time estimates of a Gantt chart (a time calendar for a particular project). This combination of DELTA and Gantt charts gives the project manager a most precise tool for managing the research project.

Thus the decision to use the DELTA chart as a control instrument by the researcher does not exclude the use of important methodologies from such other network techniques as PERT and Gantt.

A hypothetical research project is shown in a DELTA chart format in Figure 7.8. The chart has been abbreviated for space purposes.

CONCLUSIONS

Although DELTA may provide the project manager with better planning and monitoring capabilities for his communication research project, the strongest advantage of the DELTA chart is its usefulness as a communication tool. Functioning in this capacity the DELTA chart provides the project manager with a visual overview of the entire project. Shown graphically are the necessary activities and events, critical decision points with clear understanding of who is responsible, precise time estimates, and common symbols for the necessary elements.

For long, complex projects DELTA is superior to other network techniques through its increased flexibility (allowing for alternatives) for planning and its decision and logic elements. Such projects may also employ several organizations or persons and it is imperative that they see how they must function together to complete the project. DELTA is an excellent medium for communicating this interdependency.

In short, for the communication researcher serving as project manager the DELTA chart as presented here provides a number of increased capabilities. DELTA makes it possible to

plan in advance the research design of the project's objectives; predict the time required to complete the project;

spell out the research activities, events, and decision points and de-
    termine responsibilities;
provide alternatives for the research activities;
measure performance against the project plan;
control the project's progress through feedback;
use the instrument as a communication medium for all those involved.

Although language (in the form of written narratives-reports,
plans, and so on) is the chief medium for communicating information
about research projects, it is also a limited medium for conveying
information. A growing body of research expertise requires a more
precise language capable of communicating more information, but
with increased fidelity. New elements of such a communication medium are needed. Graphic communication, as represented by the
DELTA chart, is clearly a step in this direction.

REFERENCES

Holloman, H. J. 1965. "Science and Innovation." In Economics of
    Research and Development, ed. Richard A. Tybout. Columbus:
    Ohio State University Press.

Sipper, D. 1970. "Planning with Project Decision Networks." Pro-
    ceedings of the Second Annual Seminar/Symposium of Project
    Management Institute, Drexel Hill, Pa., October.

8

The Delphi Technique

Any observer of the contemporary world has no doubt noticed the time lag between the occurrence of the societal problem, the policy implemented to solve or deal with it, and the actual effect of the policy on the problem. The current energy crisis in the United States and Europe serves as a grim example. It is obvious that this problem will not be solved in the short run regardless of the policy designed to cope with it. This means that most of our policies and methodologies for generating solutions must consider the long rather than the short run. Energy policies must take into account future conditions or variables if they are to be effective. A policy that attempts to get the nation ready for any energy crisis may find that the world's energy needs and assorted problems in the future may not have been incorporated in the original policy. In fact, it may be much better to try to estimate certain future events (probabilities) about energy—for example, oil reserves, rates of consumer and industrial consumption, and so on—and base policies on these estimates.

The difficulty becomes a paradox. How does one estimate or describe a future that obviously has not occurred? In short, the policy maker is asked to become a forecaster of things to come.

The typical behavior of a policy maker who is faced with making a decision on an issue in which he lacks understanding is to rely on the judgements of experts. This method of operation is fine unless the experts disagree, and now the policy maker is in trouble again. He must now decide between opposing viewpoints or find some way to get the experts to agree. Essentially he must reduce the uncertainty to unity. Usually the policy maker given this situation will call a meeting or hold a conference in order to reach some agreement on what he should do. However, what usually happens is that some compromise decision is reached after long and often heated arguments.

Unfortunately, the policy maker does not get what he really wants, a consensus among the experts; instead he gets a compromise decision that probably none of the experts really support.

It is likely that this compromise situation results from interpersonal communication variables. The complex crisis is soon forgotten and personalities and egos emerge as the real difficulty in the meeting. The compromise may result not from objective reasoning but from all sorts of hidden agendas; for example, who is the most stubborn, talks the longest and quite possibly the loudest, or perhaps levels of power and authority get in the way of reason.

Fortunately, a more systematic method of consulting expert opinion that tends to eliminate interpersonal bias is available to the policy maker. It is a social science methodology known as the Delphi technique.

WHAT IS THE DELPHI TECHNIQUE?

The Delphi technique is a forecasting methodology for generating expert opinion on any given subject. The Rand Corporation in California developed Delphi as an attempt to eliminate interpersonal interactions as the controlling variables, as usually happens when groups of experts interact in meetings. It was named for the Greek oracle at Apollo's shrine at Delphi. At Rand the Delphi technique was originally developed to help the U.S. military make more accurate forecasts for long-range decisions. Today Delphi has been used in many planning situations—such as business, science, and government—to generate policy options, measure the impact of such options, and identify market conditions for industry. According to Olaf Helmer, coinventor of the Delphi technique, it is a methodology suitable to any problem and subsequent policy making requiring expert judgment as a necessary input.

By eliminating personal interaction, for example, face-to-face discussion in a conference room, the expert can express his or her viewpoints with anonymity. Delphi thus insures a low-risk or threat-free environment since questionnaires are the only means of communication among the experts.

The mode of communication among the experts is quite important for its subsequent effects on the participants. Feedback does occur as the opinions or judgments of the experts are systematically collected, tabulated, and then returned in the form of feedback. The responses are returned, but the author is never identified.

What is important here in our early discussion of the Delphi technique is that the reader understand the importance of communication in attacking any complex problem. The conceptual difficulty, as noted in Chapter 3, may likely prove to be more difficult than the inherent qualities of the problem per se. In other words, what is the most effective form of communication to use when analyzing the problem? Social science research literature is full of barriers to communication in different situations, but this will not be reviewed here. The Delphi technique is an attempt to overcome or eliminate one of the more severe barriers, the interpersonal interactions in a communicative situation. In this situation, the communication often becomes structured due to the wills of the personalities involved. Delphi provides the individual expert with the greatest degree of freedom from this artifact through the promise of anonymity. Thus the primary objective of Delphi is not to produce "right" answers as much as it is to produce a communication climate most conducive for rational and objective thought.

Typically, Delphi begins with a questionnaire mailed to the "experts" or respondents,who remain anonymous to each other. The experts produce their answers and return them to the principal investigator. The answers are collated and returned to each respondent. The expert is asked if he wants to change any of his answers. Usually in this round the respondents are asked to rank order some responses according to some laid-out criteria. Again, these responses are collected, tabulated, and returned to the experts. Now in this round if a respondent's estimate falls outside the interquartile range of answers, he is asked to justify or give the reasons for his answer. Usually a consensus is reached among respondents for a given set of events or items.

In summary, Delphi uses written answers rather than placing experts together in a face-to-face meeting or conference. This is helpful when the experts cannot get together physically as, say, in a study in which experts are widely scattered throughout the country or do not have time for lengthy meetings. More important, the written anonymity prevents domination by certain individuals in the group setting. It can also be useful in situations where the respondents are hostile to one another. The author, for example, has used Delphi on a research project involving police, gang members, and school officials.

HISTORY OF THE DELPHI TECHNIQUE

In the early 1950s Rand Corporation conducted research on the use of group opinion in forecasting, usually in the form of face-to-face committee discussions to develop group opinion. The research tended to confirm the well-known disadvantages of the committee approach: intense social pressure to go along with the majority; strong vocal minority opinions overriding the majority; a reluctance to get involved in a conflict leading to an agreement for agreement's sake; personality clashes; hesitation to disagree with a superior or perceived authority; and finally an undue emphasis on trying to change viewpoints. The data from the research supported the conclusion that the committee approach to forecasting produced inaccurate results. This conclusion led the Rand researchers to investigate the idea of developing forecasts leading to a consensus without the face-to-face committee discussion. This resulted in the invention of the Delphi technique.

The method was first designed by Dalkey and Helmer (1963). In a later paper Helmer (1967) emphasized the need for accurate forecasting as a planning aid for decision makers in the public and private sectors. The paper addressed in some detail the Delphi technique.

This paper was followed by a more detailed technical article authored by Dalkey (1967) and published by Rand. The paper concluded that Delphi was somewhat more accurate than committee discussions.

The first comprehensive technical paper on Delphi was published by Brown (1968) and is of particular importance because it presents a concise summary of the development, previous applications, and steps in running a Delphi.. The paper summarized six previous experiments with the Delphi technique.

In the spring of 1968 Dalkey and other researchers at Rand began a series of ten experiments dealing with factual (quantitative) judgments to further verify the Delphi technique (Dalkey 1969).

The foregoing publications suggest that prior to 1969 experiments with the Delphi technique utilized easily quantifiable data to test and develop the method. As the Rand Corporation researchers gained confidence in Delphi in the area of factual judgment, they began to expand the method into the area of value judgment. Rescher (1969) published the first technical paper on the application of Delphi in the value judgment area. Following this, the first experiment to develop and analyze value judgment of a group was conducted by Dalkey and Rourke (1971).

One of the first applications of Delphi to a practical problem was made by Dalkey and Helmer (1962). The researchers utilized Delphi to develop a consensus on an optimal industrial target system for nuclear weapons. The Delphi panel was made up of seven experts. A total of five iterations was used with the written questionnaires so structured that the answers could be easily quantified. The results indicated a definite convergence of opinion.

In the preceding sections of this chapter I have discussed in brief fashion significant Delphi research leading to the current state of the art. The Delphi technique has thus evolved as an intuitive methodology for collecting and sharing expert opinion about future events. As noted above, its original use was to develop military events through the estimates of several experts. Today Delphi is used in business and government sectors to make policy decisions.

Delphi has these distinct characteristics: anonymity of panelist response, controlled feedback, and statistical group response. These characteristics were adopted to reduce the influence of strong vocal minority, strong social pressures, and the bandwagon effect of majority opinion normally experienced in the group discussion. Out of the historical research these conclusions may be drawn concerning procedures: three to five iterations (rounds) are satisfactory to develop group consensus; and ten to 30 experts on a panel are sufficient and manageable.

Finally it is interesting to note that the historical development of Delphi has pushed beyond the confirmation of "factual" data into the realm of "judgmental" data. This is probably natural since when we make forecasts about future events we must do so without detailed factual knowledge. Such an exercise must then rely on judgment. There is a parallel here to the role of the critic in judging a work of art. He makes value judgments about the painting or film or whatever, and this judgment can be accepted or rejected by you, but his statement does not really affect the "truth" of the art object. And in scientific research the role of judgment continues as one does not really "prove" the truth of the research hypothesis as much as one is able to reject the null hypothesis. Thus Delphi is not as unique an instrument for its use of judgmental data as might first appear. All science begins in philosophy, hence, judgment.

DELPHI PROCEDURES

Typically, the Delphi technique proceeds in the following steps.

Step 1: Develop the Delphi question. This is the crucial step where the broad open-ended question is first asked. Basically the researcher is asking, "What is it I want to learn from the respondents?" Often the final question's form will be much different from the original question. In many ways this step is similar to formulating the main research hypothesis.

Step 2: Select the panel of experts. A suitable set of specialists is selected whose expert judgments are to be elicited. Depending on the complexity of the problem, usually ten to 30 are sufficient. The term "expert" simply means someone who is familiar with the stated problem. This could mean students, teachers, educational administrators, and so on, if the subject were secondary education. The main point in picking the panel of experts is that they have information to share, are motivated to work on the problem, and have the time to complete the tasks involved with the procedure.

The size of the panel depends on the complexity of the problem and the similarities of the people in the expert population. The historical literature suggested a panel of ten to 30. If the expert population is quite homogeneous, then a small panel can be used. Delbecq (1975) has noted that few new ideas are produced within a homogeneous group after the panel reaches 30. The Delphi technique can be quite time consuming, so the smaller the panel the better.

Step 3: Develop the Delphi questionnaire. Generally the questionnaire is very unstructured or open-ended. One does not want to limit in any way the range of answers from the experts. I have found in my use of Delphi that a questionnaire used for the first time in this round is best if all questions are open-ended. This gives maximum freedom to the expert, and it allows for different interpretations of the question. Later the answers can be forced into a set of categories.

Step 4: Analyze the first questionnaire. By this round the questionnaires have been returned and are now ready for analysis. Essentially the researcher must now code all responses and develop categories for the answers.

Step 5: Develop second questionnaire. The objective here is to have the panel members review the answers generated by the first questionnaire. Usually panel members are now asked to rank order preliminary priorities among the responses. For example, suppose question 1 generated a range of ten answers in the form of statements. These ten statements are printed on the second questionnaire and the panel members are asked to assign a "1" to the statement they most agree with and a "10" to the statement they least agree with. These rankings are then returned to the researcher.

Step 6: Develop third questionnaire. In this round the communication between panel members begins as the results of the second questionnaire are given to each panel member. The response rankings are made known (although no panel member is identified through his rankings or responses) and a response distribution is usually presented in terms of the median and the first and third quartiles. Panel members are asked to vote again on the ranks of the items and in those cases where the new response is outside the interquartile range (that is, the middle half of the second questionnaire), the panel member is asked to provide a statement of the reason why he or she gave an answer that differed that much from the answers supplied by the majority.

Step 7: Develop fourth questionnaire. The resulting response distribution is fed back, along with a summary of the arguments defending relatively deviant positions. Again the panel members are asked for reestimates. This time, if an answer lies outside the new interquartile range, a response in the form of a counterargument is requested stating why the majority argument in favor of a different answer was not persuasive.

Step 8: Develop final questionnaire. Again, the new answers along with the response distribution are fed back to the panel members and a final set of answers is requested, based on all the arguments and counterarguments that were presented.

Step 9: Analyze results. The medians of the responses of this final round are accepted as the group's position, representing the nearest thing to a consensus on the problem.

Step 10: Prepare a final report. The final report should indicate the spread of opinions, consensus answers, and minority arguments in defense of deviant responses. The report should be aimed at two audiences: the panel members and the policy maker who may use the results for decision making. What Delphi has done is to create a position statement for the policy maker provided he agrees with the expert consensus.

STATISTICAL TECHNIQUES

A brief note may be necessary on statistical techniques for analyzing the Delphi responses. If the responses constitute nominal data the appropriate statistical measurements are mode and frequency. If the data involve rankings or ordinal data then the appropriate statistics are median and percentile. If the data appear or are assumed to be interval then the statistical measurements are mean and standard deviation.

MAJOR ADVANTAGES

The Delphi technique offers several advantages over other ways of eliciting judgmental data.

It tends to reduce the tendency to follow the leader and lessens the bandwagon effect so common in group settings.

It focuses attention on the issue and reduces the tendency for members to get the group sidetracked.

It allows "experts" who have no history of communicating to be able to communicate due to the lack of face-to-face interaction.

It allows panel members to communicate without actually having to get together physically.

It reduces or eliminates entirely the possibility of a dominant personality controlling the outcome of the group.

It produces a threat-free environment for an individual to state his opinion.

It provides a communication structure in which everyone has a chance to be heard equally.

It provides controlled feedback to the respondents.

It is economically productive because experts do not have to be brought together and housed in order to interact.

It generates a wide range of responses, thereby assisting in trying to describe future events.

It is a technique that is usually enjoyed by the participants because of the responses that are fed back to them.

It does not require elaborate procedures to conduct.

DELPHI USES

As noted in the beginning of the chapter, a policy maker when faced with a decision in which he or she lacks technical expertise must rely on the informed judgments of experts in the area. Delphi replaces the committee with a systematic means of collection, analysis, and evaluation of the judgments of a group of experts. Delphi can aid the policy maker by obtaining a consensus or a lot of information from informed persons.

Although originally developed as a technique for long-range forecasting, Delphi today has been successfully used in other sectors and for other purposes. These include:

Building a model of a complex problem by eliciting statements of structure and process of it.

Laying out the positive and negative aspects of a crucial decision that has to be made.

Revealing causal relationships between events.

Measuring the impacts of a particular policy on other variables in the problem.

Constructing theory through a series of statements about the most significant research finds in the field.

Identifying barriers to the implementation of a particular policy.

Identifying future market conditions for industry.

As a research tool for examining history or past performance.

As a beginning point for implementing zero-based budgeting.

Some of the above uses of Delphi may be obvious, but some of them should be spelled out in more detail.

In measuring the impacts of a particular policy on other variables in the problem. The aim is to view the phenomenon in a system. This means that it may have many parts that are not evident at first glance. Many failures in the business world result from a neglect of this type of reasoning. So the trick is to do something of a minisimulation and say, "What if we implemented Policy A?" Each expert then attempts to measure the impact (positive, neutral, or negative) of this policy on events or parts of the phenomenon with which he is familiar. This use of Delphi illustrates that the goal is not always consensus. The goal may be simply to state all the pros and cons for a particular policy. Even if a policy maker has already reached a decision to implement Policy A, it may be to his advantage to explore all the negative reactions that will occur after his decision is known.

Delphi has been used to explore causal relationships in complex phenomena. It has been the author's experience that the exploration of causality is particularly fruitful when Delphi is used, followed by the use of the cross-impact analysis technique discussed in the next chapter. Briefly, in the cross-impact technique a matrix is built consisting of causal (it is assumed) events and the user is asked to assign probabilities or estimates of the impact one event will have on another. The list of events to be cross impacted is generated by Delphi.

An organization might not be doing well in one of its particular product lines or a service clinic may have failed to reach a particular population; such problems could be explored with Delphi by looking at the history of these failures. Past events could be generated by a Delphi panel of those most directly involved in the efforts producing an excellent and useful historical record. From this record, reasons for the failure might be identified.

It is doubtful if any professional would seriously make the claim that he or she has read all the relevant scholarly and research literature of the past decade in his field. If theory is built up "event by event," or "research finding after research finding," then it is impossible for one individual to consider everything (research findings) relevant to theory construction. However, a group of experts, professionals in the field, could through the use of Delphi come much closer to considering all of the relevant findings for the past decade.

Finally in the application of Delphi to the now-popular zero-based budgeting concept it would appear payoff is possible. In zero-based budgeting each person submitting a budget to the central office must assume he starts with no money and must make the case for his budget. With Delphi, each person could comment on the other budget requests, with an overall understanding of the organization's total budget and a better understanding of how and why the final allocations were made. Charges of personal bias and other grumblings could be lessened because Delphi would make every argument for every allocation known.

Delphi has recently been used in planning exercises. Panel members have been asked to generate postures or behaviors that might be utilized either to enhance or reduce the probability that an event would occur. For example, if one were trying to reduce vandalism in public schools, the superintendent might ask the panel of experts to produce or comment on intervention strategies for reducing the level of vandalism.

Or, an education administrator at the Department of Health, Education and Welfare might use a Delphi panel to improve educational policies and generate alternative future options for coping with problems. In such forecasting use of Delphi, the technique is also valuable in spelling out the underlying assumptions concerning the probabilities of occurrence of future events. Speculation about future events can be very hazy, but Delphi tends to flush out the assumptions of the respondents, making the future clearer.

As an educational planning tool, Delphi was used by the staff from the Institute for the Future and the Educational Policy Research Center, Syracuse University Research Corporation (Gordon 1968) to make forecasts about the future of education.

Delphi was again used in a study by the Institute for the Future sponsored by the Syracuse Educational Policy Research Center (Brigard 1970) to develop long-range forecasts based on social indicators such as urbanization, international relations, conflict in society and law enforcement, national political structure, values and the impact of technology on government and society. The study did not attempt to develop a detailed description of the future, but it sought to articulate expectations about the future by experts in the social sciences.

Delphi has been used in a number of other settings as well, including such divergent subjects as educational reform, long-range corporate planning, in medicine to obtain estimates of current rates of disease incidence, assessments regarding the quality of life, governmental planning, and estimating crime statistics.

DELPHI AS A TEACHING AID

As has been noted in previous chapters, one of the great difficulties in thinking about complex social problems is their inherent complexity. The use of Delphi in numerous settings strongly suggests that it is a potent teaching methodology or tool. An array of events related to the problem under study tends to form (as called for in Chapter 3) a gestalt for those examining it. The bottom line of this is that Delphi is capable of teaching someone to think concretely about complex phenomena. For a policy maker this is likely to mean a better decision will be reached because many facets of the problem have been explored and alternative consequences of various policies have been examined.

In a sense, Delphi can be construed as an anonymous debate, in that the experts are aware of the opinions of the others and are asked to respond to them without knowing the authors' identity. But the knowledge of the differences of opinion held by those who hold different positions (technical and managerial functions) is a valuable planning aid for the policy maker in that it suggests different strategies for persuading various groups to follow the conclusions of the Delphi. One group might be convinced of the conclusions on, say, protection of the environment, while another group may be more convinced that the exploration of energy reserves deserves top priority. Different strategies to marshal the support of both groups are required. Diffusion studies offer real-world examples of the failure to predict important intervening variables and develop alternative strategies for implementation.

FINAL OBSERVATIONS

The ultimate welfare of any civilized society depends on how the economic, natural, moral, and intellectual resources of that society are applied to the problems that face it.

Delphi is a methodology for marshaling some of these resources via the intellectual route and then articulating how these can be applied to the problem at hand. In effect, Delphi is philosophically grounded in the notion that several minds are better than one in making subjective estimates or predictions about what should be done in the future and that "experts" or informed people, within a controlled communication environment, free of personal pressures, will make judgments based on rational thought and shared information rather than merely guessing, and that they will ultimately reach sound conclusions on which coping policies can be built.

These forecasts or predictions are not necessarily extrapolations based on current or specific conditions, but are reasoned estimates of future conditions. The validity of such estimates cannot be based on such mathematical functions as a Poisson curve or Baumon's law. Their validity must be measured by reason or grounded in existing theory, models, logic, or arguments of deduction.

However, given the complex problems that confront us and the fact that no single individual can be fully informed about his discipline and the interdisciplinary nature of societal issues, it is necessary to find some way to utilize expert knowledge. To do this, it is necessary to find some way to enable the experts to communicate, so that information can be drawn from them individually. In short, to aim the intellectual resources squarely at the problem, a way, as in Delphi, must be found that assures effective communication among the experts. In a complex problem the possibility of miscommunication is infinite because even if an expert has a good grasp on how to solve the problem, the difficulty in explaining that to others and their subsequent interpretation may lead to misunderstanding.

Because many of our societal problems are novel and have never been dealt with before and therefore have no historical record, it is apparent that our problem-solving attempts must emphasize explanation so that the credibility and plausibility of the estimates can be judged.

Despite the progress with the Delphi technique, it is apparent that our ability to use our intellectual resources, or expert opinion, on current societal problems is in its infancy.

The modest success of Delphi as a methodology for problem solving and policy generation is underscored by my intuitive feeling or hunch that people can process expert advice rather well if it is given to them. The problem is the other side of the coin: the generation rather than the utilization of expert judgment. Therefore, the use of Delphi as such a generating tool—and its promise does seem far from negligible—would suggest that the pursuit of this technique is worthwhile.

REFERENCES

de Brigard, R., and Olaf Helmer. 1970. "Some Potential Societal Developments, 1970-1990." Middletown, Conn.: Institute for the Future, R-7, April.

Brown, Bernice. 1968. Delphi Process. Rand Corp. P-3925.

Dalkey, Norman. 1967. Delphi. Rand Corp. P-3704, October.

_____. 1969. The Delphi Method: An Experimental Study of Group Opinion. Rand Corp. RM-5888-PR, June.

Dalkey, Norman, and Olaf Helmer. 1962. "An Experimental Application of the Delphi Method to the Use of Experts." Rand Corp. RM-727, July.

_____. 1963. "An Experimental Application of the Delphi Method to the Use of Experts." Management Science 9.

Dalkey, Norman, and D. Rourke. 1971. Experimental Assessment of Delphi Procedures with Group Value Judgments. Rand Corp. R-612-ARPA, February.

Delbecq, Andre. 1975. Group Techniques for Program Planning. Glenview, Ill.: Scott, Foresman.

Gordon, T. J., and R. Sahr. 1968. "Report on Forecasts of Educational Administration." Middletown, Conn.: Institute for the Future, September.

Helmer, Olaf. 1967. Analysis of the Future: The Delphi Method. Rand Corp. P-3553, March.

Rescher, N. 1969. Delphi and Values. Rand Corp. P-3182, September.

9

Cross-Impact Analysis

As has been noted in earlier chapters, one of the more difficult problems in trying to solve societal difficulties stems from the interdependence of social elements. This conceptual problem soon turns into a communication one as well. The conceptual difficulty immediately arises when we try to organize the large amounts of data connected with any social issue. Our particular methodology usually falls short of the complexity involved. Second, it is hard if not almost impossible to plot the numerous cause and effect stimuli. Traditional methodology is just not suitable to reveal the web of interdependencies in a clear, concise, and systematic fashion, say for the natural gas shortage and its subsequent effects on society. Such traditional methodology is almost always doomed to failure because it is linear, reduced to parts, and is too narrow, while the real-world problem is nonlinear, systemic, and consequently general in scope.

However, there is a fairly new methodology, cross-impact analysis, that attempts to cope with the conceptual and communication obstacles found in typical societal problems.

WHAT IS CROSS-IMPACT ANALYSIS?

Cross-impact analysis is a methodology for revealing and examining the interactions among future events. Its purpose is to identify events that will either aid or hinder the occurrence of other events; in short, to determine cause and effect relationships.

One of the reasons cross-impact analysis is particularly suited to this is that it constructs a matrix of all events relevant to the problem under examination. From a communication perspective, the matrix is much more comprehensible than a linear account (such

132

as a journal article or report) when one is trying to grasp an overview of the problem.

The cross-impact concept originated with Olaf Helmer and Theodore Gordon in conjunction with the design of a forecasting game for Kaiser-Aluminum and represented an effort to extend the forecasting techniques of the Delphi method. This first cross-impact analysis thus occurred in 1966, and in 1968 at UCLA, T. J. Gordon and H. Hayward developed a computer-based approach to cross-impact analysis. In this approach, events were recorded on an orthogonal matrix and at each intersection the question was asked: "If the event in the row were to occur, how would it affect the probability of occurrence of the event in the column?" Then the judgments were entered in the matrix cells.

It is interesting to point out here that most forecasting methods, as noted earlier in the chapter on the Delphi method, often run the risk that reactions between forecasted events may not be fully considered. Cross-impact analysis, however, attempts to reveal the conditional probability of an event given that various other events have or have not occurred.

As General Systems Theory has taught us, societal events do not occur in isolation, but are in some way connected to other events and developments. From a process perspective, it is difficult to imagine a societal issue that does not have roots intertwined with antecedent events or conditions and, in addition, does not affect in some way future events or conditions. Hence the term "cross impact" forms something of a gestalt. Pardee (1967) has noted, "Of all the methodological issues facing the technological forecaster, the problem of interdependencies is probably the most vexing." Kahn and Weiner (1967) have also noted:

> The interacting effects (among forecasted items) tend to be important not only because advances in one area are correlated with or spur advances in other areas, but also because various separate advances often allow for unexpected solutions to problems, or can be fitted together to make new wholes that are greater than the sum of their parts, or lead to other unexpected innovations.

In essence, cross-impact analysis attempts to uncover the conditional probabilities of forecasted events in a set along with identifying the potential interactions among them.

CROSS-IMPACT MATRIXES

The matrix as developed in a cross-impact analysis offers a systematic way of illustrating the interdependent nature of events. Consider the matrix below:

	E_1	E_2	E_3	E_n
E_1				
E_2				
E_3				
E_n				

For example, the cell at the intersection of the Event 1 (E_1) row and Event 3 (E_3) column tells the reader how the occurrence of E_1 will affect the probability of occurrence of E_3. While the cell entries reflect expert judgment, once the matrix has been completed it can be used to trace the cross impacts of any given event. In other words, a network of interdependencies can be constructed following a single event through the matrix. In cross-impact analysis the matrix soon becomes something of a model or theory concerning the interactions of a given set of events. For one attempting to cope with a complex social issue, whether from a research or policy-making position, the early construction of a model or theory to serve as a map for the analysis is most welcome. Particularly when dealing with a novel or exceedingly complex problem a model or theory is usually not available.

Certainly one of the more important objectives of the cross-impact analysis is to build an explicit model or theory which then can be used to test solutions or policies that would, in effect, either improve or decrease the probability of occurrence of events associated with the problem at hand. The matrix insures that all interactions between the set of events will be defined and their probability of occurrence estimated.

Judgment is obviously necessary to estimate the expected probabilities, but with the matrix such judgments are stated out in the open for everyone to see rather than hidden in some long statement full of jargon. Only the naive assume social issues do not contain subjective evaluations that ultimately, in a democracy, become political. The matrix of the cross-impact analysis simply forces these judgments into the light much sooner than they might normally be. Because of this the matrix serves a broad public rather than a private one, and the judgments that go into the matrix estimates are open to public question and discussion. In addition, these judgments easily can be modified to reflect more and better information as it becomes available.

With these judgments about event interactions before our eyes, a large number of scenarios can be analyzed to measure the consequences of suggested solutions or policies. It is important to recall that the Delphi method and the cross-impact technique are often used together to form an analysis. The expert panel forming the Delphi group can then be used to supply the probability estimates for the events along with the actual event identification.

A final point about the matrix is that each of the cells (interactions) can be viewed as a hypothesis for further testing. Through such hypothesis formation sometimes hidden multiple linkages are made explicit for the researcher or policy maker.

One of the key outcomes of cross-impact analysis is the identification of unknown linkages or effects among events. The method identifies not only the more obvious direct effects of an event or action but also the secondary and tertiary effects as well. Consider this example by Coates (1971). The introduction of the automobile provides people with a means of traveling rapidly, easily, cheaply, privately, door to door (first-order consequence); hence, people patronize stores at greater distances from their homes; these are generally bigger stores that have large clienteles (second-order consequence); hence, residents of a community do not meet so often and therefore do not know each other so well (third-order consequence); hence, being strangers to each other, community members find it difficult to unite to deal with common problems, and individuals find themselves increasingly isolated and alienated from their neighbors (fourth-order consequence); hence, isolated from their neighbors, members of a family depend more on each other for satisfaction of their psychological needs (fifth-order consequence); hence, because spouses are unable to meet heavy psychological demands that each makes on the other, frustration occurs, which may lead to divorce (sixth-order consequence). All of the consequences are linked and do not occur in isolation, and yet their identification may not be apparent at first glance.

CROSS-IMPACT QUESTIONS

The first question to be asked in the construction of a cross-impact matrix is: "What is the probability that an event, x, will occur before some specified future point in time?" After these estimates are recorded the second essential question for the matrix construction is: "What is your estimate that event x will occur, if it is certain that event y will occur before the specified point in time in question one?"

Certainly the first question generates a probabilistic model for the occurrence of certain events, but with the assumption of the second question, the estimator is now asked to create a new set of transition probabilities. These answers could be viewed as "causal" probabilities from which one would hope to glean "correlation coefficients" and thereby have some tentative measure of the degree of causal impact one event has upon another.

CROSS IMPACTS

Assume that a set of events has been estimated to have occurred before some future time period, with varying levels of probability. If we call these events E_1, E_2, E_3, E_n with associated probabilities P_1, P_2, P_3, P_n then the question can be asked: If E_1 ($P_1 = 100\%$) has occurred, how do the probabilities (P_2, P_3, P_n) of the other events change? Generally we will see the individual event probabilities change either positively or negatively with the occurrence or nonoccurrence of other events. An event's probability can remain the same, but this is not likely.

For example, assume the following events and probabilities were forecast for a given year:

Event	Probability
1. Reliable energy consumption estimates for all winter months	.50
2. New sources of natural gas discovered	.20
3. Energy usage levels cut by one-fourth	.30
4. Alternative form of energy developed	.10

Under cross-impact analysis this can be put in matrix form:

If this event were to occur	then probability of			
	E_1	E_2	E_3	E_n
E_1		×	×	×
E_2	×		−	×
E_3	+	×		×
E_n	×	×	−	

Thus if E_3, "energy usage levels cut by one-fourth," were to occur, E_1, "reliable energy consumption estimates for all winter months," would become more probable as noted by the plus sign in the interaction cell. On the other hand, if E_2, "new sources of natural gas discovered," occurred, E_3, "energy usage levels cut by one-fourth," would become less probable as noted by the minus sign in the cell. No impact is indicated by the × in the cell.

STEPS IN MAKING THE CROSS-IMPACT MATRIX

Step 1: Identify the set of events that is relevant to the problem at hand. The events may be actions, decisions, goals, objectives, and evaluation components, such as profits, scores on an examination, and so on.

Step 2: State the length of the time period for which events may be considered (one year, six months, and so on), and indicate if the time period is to be broken down into intervals for planning purposes. For example, if one were using cross-impact analysis to evaluate the effects of new crime-prevention methods in a city, one might decide to look at the entire system every three months for a year. Through this form of quarterly feedback we can adjust our initial probabilities to reflect what is actually happening in the real-world system.

Step 3: For each time period estimate for each event, E_i, the probability, P_i, that it will occur during the time period specified. (It is assumed that the event has not already occurred, because cross-impact analysis is concerned only with forecasting future events as it is a planning methodology.) The estimates for each of the events usually come from intuitive judgments by experts or from the Delphi method. If one has time series data then existing extrapolation models can be used to get the estimates.

Step 4: For each event, E_i, estimate how much its occurrence or nonoccurrence at a specified time would increase or decrease the probabilities of the subsequent occurrence of other events. Now enter this informationin a cross-impact matrix.

Step 5: Determine if the matrix is "balanced." This can be accomplished by "playing" the matrix a sufficiently large number of times (preferably on a computer):

Begin with the given event probabilities for the first time interval, and through a random device determine which of the events are occurring in the first time interval.
Change the subsequent event probabilities for each of the events based on the occurrence of events.
Calculate the deviations the events show from their anticipated probabilities before the matrix was played.
Record event probabilities for a large number of runs (usually 100), compute the average number of occurrences and compare these with those originally estimated.

Step 6: Conduct a sensitivity analysis. Change the initial or original probability estimates of the events, E_i, one at a time, by some amount (usually 10 or 20 percent) and then play the matrix to determine how much, on the average, the probabilities for each event are affected by this change.

Step 6 is an important one from a policy-making perspective because this analysis should reveal which events are most easily affected by different conditions and which events offer the most leverage in affecting other events. Usually it becomes quite apparent after the matrix has been played that some events cause significant changes in the overall matrix while other events seem to have about the same impact regardless of their probability of occurrence. This information enables the planner or policy maker to identify or develop promising strategies (promoting the occurrence of a particular event) for dealing with the problem. Figure 9.1 is a partial matrix.

FIGURE 9.1
Results of Cross-Impact Analysis
(100 runs)

Event	Original Probability	Modified Probability
1. College enrollments up for 1976	.90	.80
2. Enrollment of minorities up	.70	.60
3. Enrollment of veterans up	.60	.40
4. More new instructors needed	.30	.10

Source: Compiled by the author.

Playing the matrix reveals that several events are not as probable as had previously been estimated based on the judgments of our college administrators. The interactions or cross impacts between events result in different probabilities of occurrence. In the sensitivity analysis (Step 6) Event 3 was decreased by one-third (which is actually what happened in the fall of 1976) with the subsequent decrease in probability of Events 1, 2, and 4. The cross-impact linkages thus suggest a "sneak preview" of what implications may be in store for college enrollments. The loss or drop in veterans' enrollment followed the expiration of GI Bill benefits for more than 3.3 million veterans in June 1976.

The matrix illustrates the use of cross-impact analysis to test the expected, or in this example to consider an institution's policy on hiring new instructors for the coming academic year. Clearly, the results are that fewer instructors will be needed. Such an interaction is revealed by playing out the matrix in accordance with techniques (quadratic equation) described by Gordon and Hayward (1968).

SUBJECTIVE PROBABILITIES

When the person or panel has agreed upon a list of relevant events, they must then forecast for each event over some specific time period the probabilities of occurrence. In instructing them, I have found it useful to ask them to think of the probabilities using a subjective scale, particularly if they are not used to thinking in terms of probabilities, such as:

	Percent
Very likely	90–100
Likely	70–90
As likely as not	50
Not very likely	10–30
Unlikely	0–10

Policy-making planners may want to use the following subjective scales for measuring the impact of a particular decision or policy:

Critical	necessary for success
Major	almost necessary for success
Significant	helpful but not necessary for success
Slight	a noticeable or enhancing effect

Such scales, while subjective, can be very useful in translating the numbers in the matrix to something meaningful for people who are not used to working with numbers. The appropriate place for the last scale is in Step 6, sensitivity analysis, when the common question is, "What does the matrix tell us?"

TIME SEQUENCE OF EVENTS

The careful reader will have noted by now that there are some events that will not or cannot occur before some other "critical" event has occurred. For example, electrical energy produced by atomic power cannot occur until a nuclear power plant has been built. Likewise, permission to build the plant must come before either event. Other events may appear at any time, such as a change in market conditions or the election of an official with a particular philosophy for dealing with the problem under study.

Gordon and Hayward (1968) offer three modes of connections or adjectives for describing the interactions between events. These modes are unrelated, enhancing, and inhibiting. For instance, assume event E_1 occurs. Event E_2 may be unaffected by E_1; it may be enhanced by the occurrence of E_1; or it may be inhibited by the occurrence of E_1. Thus with enhancing linkages, the probability of the second event is increased by the occurrence of the first. With inhibiting linkages, the probability of the second event is decreased by the occurrence of the first. The expansion of air flights to most cities and towns inhibited the further development of the train as a means of national transportation for people.

Enzer (1975) has offered a modified approach of the cross-impact model by dividing the events into three time periods: near, intermediate, and long term. Four types of subsets of events are built into the time frames: (1) events that may occur in the same time interval, but not in any special sequence (these events may not be causally related); (2) events that can only occur in a specific sequence, such as Event X must come before Event Y could occur; (3) events that are likely to occur in a sequence due to time of occurrence; and (4) alternative events—similar events where the occurrence of one usually inhibits the other. Partitioning of the events is shown below:

Near term	Intermediate	Long term
Events 1-6	Events 7-16	Events 17-24

Enzer reports that the partitioning of the events into these time frames and subsets is necessary for the realism of the matrix but that it also reduces the number of needed inputs (events) significantly. For instance, if a sequence of events is believed to be implausible, there is no need to collect the information and obtaining it is time consuming. Another important advantage to this procedure is that the chance of an input error such as double accounting is reduced. Enzer has field tested this procedure in an industrial setting and found it reliable and the results realistic.

THEORETICAL ADVANTAGES

All research and most attempts at problem solving require factual data and judgments. Often the judgments get translated into "facts" or get buried in a pile of assumptions. From an end-results point of view as well as producing good theory, these necessary judgments need to be made explicit. They need to be out in the open for everyone concerned to examine.

Fortunately cross-impact analysis makes such judgments quite explicit. The events and their associated probabilities are stated graphically in the form of a matrix. The matrix, serving as a communication medium, illustrates rather vividly the arguments in Chapter 3 for a new way of expressing complexity. The matrix makes the judgments visible and denies the possibility of their being glossed over.

Related to the explicit exposure of the judgments is the heuristic nature of the cross-impact matrix. The listing of elements or events relevant to the problem at hand does seem to trigger additional thinking as to what other events might be included in the analysis. In addition, the cross impacts or interactions between events also serve a heuristic function in that linkages, causal and correlational, perhaps never noticed before, are now recognized. The strengths of the interactions can be estimated through descriptors and probabilities for additional insights.

The cross-impact method makes it possible to integrate the opinions of experts possibly from different disciplines because they are asked to provide judgments about the problem under study. The recording of these judgments in the appropriate matrix cells thus reflects the interdisciplinary flavor of cross-impact analysis. The generation of the list of events to be cross impacted also reflects the integration of various disciplines for a common end.

Finally the completed matrix may function as a model or theory for the research analysis. As noted earlier, each cell may be viewed as a potential hypothesis that is saying, "There is a relationship between E_1 and E_2." All of these taken together, if they are of sufficient magnitude, could form a low- or middle-range theory about the phenomenon under review. The hypothesis and/or theory generation capability of the cross-impact analysis method is one of its subtle but powerful attributes.

Once the matrix has been completed it can serve as a testing ground for policies. For instance, a particular policy could be added to the row of events and cross impacted through the matrix for possible effects. In essence, the cross-impact matrix allows for the simulation of policy. Obviously, any change in the matrix cells is due to the policy, and a policy maker or decision maker can consider his options with new data at hand. The Education Policy Research Center at Syracuse University has used cross-impact analysis in the formation of educational policy.

In making policy the crucial question is: "If E_1 happens, how is E_2 affected?" It is imperative to focus on the idea of mutual causality, even though we are not dealing with a precise natural science issue subject to laws. Because precise answers are usually not forthcoming for social problems, judgment is given new importance. Expert judgments are necessary if policy is to be generated and implemented. The systematic form of the cross-impact analysis matrix is of tremendous help here because it forces all participants to be explicit in their judgments about the relationships between events. The completed matrix can aid the researcher in describing and explaining the phenomenon and may even aid him in stating predictions about it. As Helmer (1973) has observed about the cross-impact method, "It is likely to emerge as a useful analytical tool in many areas, particularly in the social sciences, where there is a scarcity of methodological constructs that may be of aid in attaining theoretical generalizations."

Once the cross-impact matrix has been completed, some additional observations may be gleaned from it. The trick is to study the matrix in detail for possible "ricochet" effects, secondary and tertiary impacts, that an early glance at the matrix failed to see. These effects, while indirect rather than direct, may have such a cumulative effect on the total system that the events causing them become likely targets of intervention in order to influence other developments.

A final use of the matrix may be found in gaming theory. The idea of comparing various policy actions leads straight to the idea of a planning game or scenario. Different events can be assumed to have occurred to see how they might affect occurrences of other events. In short, a planner can use the ideas of game theory to test various alternative policies.

The operation of the cross-impact model as a one-person game can easily be changed to a two- or multiperson game, in which the inputs by several participants can be observed.

PRAGMATIC ADVANTAGES

Forecasting is a crucial step in any decision- or policy-making effort. This is particularly true for actions designed to solve societal problems when often the solution may take years to become truly effective. A policy decision to commit scarce resources to building a mass transit system for Los Angeles would likely mean that it would be years before such a system was operational. Societal decisions thus may have long time lags and far-reaching implications.

But if our problems are to be solved, such decisions have to be made. Modern decision making thus requires effective forecasting techniques such as cross-impact analysis. Such techniques as Delphi analysis, scenario writing, strategic planning, and cross-impact analysis have been used successfully in problem solving, with accurate forecasts and communication to all interested parties of the complexities involved in the problem.

Planners using the cross-impact analysis method have found it productive and operational. They have found it fruitful for producing or identifying key chains of events or miniscenarios and suggesting possible policy actions. Enzer (1975) reports on one use of the matrix that proved to be highly effective.

An efficient way to generate the list of events for the cross-impact matrix is to ask, "What would help you the most in solving the problem?" and "What would hinder you the most?"

For most problems a list of 25-50 events will usually define or identify the most relevant dimensions of a problem. In actual practice one may use the "brainstorming" technique to generate a list of 100 events, and after some hard thinking this list can usually be cut back. It is necessary to point out, however, that most of the success of cross-impact analysis rests on the careful selection of events to be cross impacted, so this process cannot be rushed. If one is going to err, it is much better to do it on the side of too many events than too few.

The cross-impact method has been used among others at Monsanto Corporation and General Electric in corporate planning and at Syracuse University and the Rand Corporation. It has been used in Belgium for developing PPBS budgets and in various Canadian government agencies.

Mansfield (1961) used cross-impact analysis to trace the spread of certain ideas from innovation within one company to use of that idea by other firms in the same sector.

Finally in the area of group management, a process in which each manager brings his own background, training, intelligence, and judgment to the problem, cross-impact analysis has been used to impose structure on an otherwise unwieldy decision-making system.

DRAWBACKS

Despite the theoretical and pragmatic advantages to cross-impact analysis as a methodology, it does have drawbacks. These need to be discussed as one is talking about applying the method to real-world social problems.

First, because the method is intended to analyze future rather than past events, it cannot rely on hard, experimental data but must use probability estimates and judgments about the future. This does not mean that harder data, when they are available, cannot be substituted into the matrix. In other words, the current state of development for any body of knowledge can be used by the cross-impact analysts as inputs. But some reliance on expert judgment is unavoidable.

Second, the amount of information that must be gathered is quite large. The cross impacts have to be estimated and just the mere collection of such estimates from a panel of experts can become a large task in itself.

Third, only pairwise interactions are taken into consideration. We know that in the real world it is often the combined interaction of three or more events that produces the final effect. It is difficult for the mind to perceive multidimensional interactions and state them in probabilistic terms.

CONCLUSIONS

Although the drawbacks exist, it remains to be seen if they are permanent deficiencies or technological shortcomings that further research will eliminate.

But the potential power of this methodology is formidable. It is content-free, allowing an unlimited selection of potential events of almost any discipline or field—institutional, technological, economic, corporate, political, goal-oriented, social. It is, then, a methodological tool for conducting analyses. The drawbacks associated with it simply reflect the complexity of the problem that is under attack.

For anyone seriously interested in problem solving, cross-impact analysis should be considered because it offers analytical techniques not usually offered in standard methodology. As a methodology its great strength rests on its ability to capture the essential aspects that affect the relationships between the components in the problem. The realism of the matrix cannot be denied.

Finally, in working in areas in which no adequate theory exists, as in complex social phenomena, the matrix forces the researchers to pay careful attention to the impacts or interactions between all events. The results of this analysis may generate a theory where before none existed.

REFERENCES

Coates, J. F. 1971. "Technology Assessment: The Benefits . . . the Costs . . . the Consequences." The Futurist 5, no. 6 (December).

Enzer, S. 1975. "The Role of Futures Research in Corporate Planning." University of Southern California, Center for Futures Research, March.

Gordon, T. J., and H. Hayward. 1968. "Initial Experiments with the Cross Impact Matrix Method of Forecasting." Futures 1.

Helmer, O. 1973. "Accomplishments and Prospects of Futures Research." University of Southern California, Center for Futures Research, August.

Kahn, H., and A. Wiener. 1967. The Year 2000. New York: Macmillan.

Mansfield, E. 1961. "Diffusion of Technological Change." Reviews of Data on Research and Development. National Science Foundation, October.

Pardee, F. S. 1967. "Technological Projection and Advanced Product Planning." Rand Corp. P-3622, July.

10
Policy Making
with Scenarios

In a recent edition of the Los Angeles Times, it was reported that a portable color television set was stolen from a home. The burglar's victim said he would not press charges because he was only interested in getting his television set back. Eventually the thief was caught by the police, but the color television had already been sold. Following the trial the criminal received a suspended sentence, but the victim was told he would have to sue the burglar in order to try to get his money back.

This incident, as reported in the press, underscores the basic problems of crime and society's inability to deter it. After more than a decade of such agencies as special police units, municipal officials, school administrators, courts, social-welfare and public-service workers, crime still remains a rampant social problem.

Specifically this story illustrates the failure of our criminal justice planning system to design policies that punish offenders as well as help victims. In practice, as reported every day in the news media, criminal penalties fail to accomplish their goals: to deter crime and rehabilitate criminals.

Very briefly, it is suggested here and will be argued later in the chapter that the failure of the criminal justice system to develop policies to achieve its goals is due to an inaccurate description of the relationship between crime and society. Planning efforts have failed to focus on the variables that control or influence criminals; instead they have focused on crime statistics (crimes rather than criminals) and are thus unable to explain fluctuations in the statistics so that, as a guide for policy, they are not very useful.

It will be argued in this chapter that a particular social science methodology, scenario construction, can be used to cope with social problems.

WHAT ARE SCENARIOS?

Scenario construction has to do with the generation of various assumptions necessary for any exercise in planning. Formally, a "scenario" can be defined as a chronological description of hypothetical events occurring in the future of a particular system. In short, scenarios attempt to describe future changes in the state or condition of a social system. In attempting to describe a future state of a system, a scenario details the conditions and events that are considered to precede a particular prediction.

In dealing with complexity the future is always uncertain. But the future is also malleable in that particular choices of action or decisions do impact upon future conditions; hence, the often quoted phrase, "You can invent the future." The construction of scenarios is aimed at determining future environments. A policy maker using the scenario technique must provide distinct and comprehensible descriptions of alternative futures.

Thus scenarios used in policy making are general descriptions of future conditions and events and related variables. The difficult part is to decide which of these elements are to be described in the scenario. This chapter will be concerned with a strategy for making those decisions.

Much of the success of scenarios as planning and policy-making tools depends on the establishment of causal linkages between elements or variables that directly affect the system under consideration and crucial external or environmental factors. If planning and policy making are based on rational thinking, it is assumed that rational thoughts are based on a consideration of all viable alternatives to the problem at hand. A scenario is constructed to flesh out these alternatives.

It is important to pause here and point out that there is nothing magic connected with scenarios. A scenario is a rigorous, rational methodology. Of course, any exercise or tool that is concerned with prediction is based on "If . . . then . . . ." type of assumptions. In other words, any scenario statement is a conditional one.

SCENARIOS AS METHODOLOGY

The scenario technique is a methodology for discovering the crucial elements of a system that actually determine its future state; combining these elements with probabilistic estimates about the likelihood of their occurrence; stating predictions about the possible futures of the system given the assumptions and particular arrangements of the key elements; and communicating the first three objectives in such a fashion that what has been done is clearly visible to anyone examining the scenario.

In short, the scenario methodology is a disciplined effort to objectively predict future conditions of a system while using rational, systematic thought processes. To oversimplify for the sake of clarity, it is a method for rigorous common sense. Quite simply, the result or product of this procedure is an estimate of the threats and opportunities facing a system (for example, organization, institution, or government) based on the conditions stated in the scenario. Given this knowledge, the system can develop policies for coping or altering such a future state so that it may operate in a less hostile environment.

The communicative qualities ot a scenario are overwhelming. The principal objective of the scenario is to provide structure for the thinking aimed at attacking the complexity. Since the future is hazy, any technique that provides some structure for storing our conjectures about it is most welcome. Consequently, if the method can provide a structure for holding our thoughts about the future, then the mind is free to examine it more critically, raise crucial questions, and hopefully raise additional insights. Since the method is as much concerned with exploring future conditions as with predicting them, the communication aspects of the technique become imperative. As a communication stimulus the scenario allows the policy maker to provoke discussions, analyze in depth specific parts of contingency plans, and establish liaison behaviors.

Generally it is convenient to divide the scenario into three sections: general and specific situations, events, and personnel behaviors.

General and specific situations are written descriptions of past and present conditions. They provide background information so that a logical hypothetical chain of events can be constructed by the scenario users. They include such information as political climate, market conditions, natural resources, technology, weather, behaviors of individuals and groups, legal requirements, and so forth—in short, any element that might affect the system.

Events describe incidents (as compared with the setting above) that require the organization to respond. For example, the scenario might begin with the organization faced with a crisis and then build to other developments in some logical time sequence. The events and time frame can be altered to evaluate aspects of the coping action (policy) and measure results.

Personnel behaviors are the actions taken by the participants in the scenario. These should always be recorded in some fashion, either taped or written, so they can be studied later for analysis. For example, if a decision is made it should be recorded. It has been my experience when using the scenario methodology that more productive results occur when the bulk of the scenario writing is done by the key policy makers under the watchful eye of the social scientist consultant. Their familiarity with their system and its environment produces a more realistic scenario, and they best know the degree of specifics needed for practical construction.

Scenarios have been used in industry as well as in governmental agencies as planning devices. Perhaps their best-known use has been by the futurist group, the Club of Rome, and by Herman Kahn in his books, Of Things to Come and The Next Two Hundred Years: A Scenario for America and the World. The Next Two Hundred Years (1976) is presented as an optimistic view to offset the pessimism of the neo-Malthusians. Kahn offers a set of four scenarios ranging from "convinced neo-Malthusian" through "guarded pessimist" and "guarded optimist" to "technology and growth enthusiast." The Educational Policy Research Center of Stanford Research Institute has used the scenario method to produce alternative, holistic, 30-year projections for the United States and project subsequent policy formation by the U.S. Office of Education. A number of major U.S. corporations have used scenarios to plan marketing strategies. Abroad, the scenario technique has been used in Europe, especially by France, and by Japan.

SCENARIO CONSTRUCTION

The construction of a scenario can best be described in six steps.

Step one: The system is defined. This usually means the organization we are interested in and the key elements we consider necessary for its description. This could mean personnel, profits, cash flows, productivity, technology, physical plant, laws, operating rules, learning curves, test scores, and so on. In essence, an operational definition of the system.

Step two: A time period is established for the system to operate. The scenario begins with the present situation and then varies in length for future years. Usually the time period covered is five to 30 years if the objective is to obtain fairly specific predictions. Certainly the time period can be much longer if the research question demands it.

Step three: Obviously the system in our scenario does not operate or exist in isolation. By definition it is an open rather than a closed system so it is surrounded by an environment that impacts upon it. The environment may be physical as represented by geographical boundaries or weather conditions, or it may be of a different dimension as in social, economic, psychological, communicative, or military contexts. The point here is to identify the external constraints of the environment on the system. One must resist the temptation to define the environment too broadly. There is a tendency for social scientists to do this and, hence, confuse the system with the environment. The productivity of the scenario depends on a relatively uncomplicated set of descriptions. The crucial elements of the environment should be viewed as givens as one would assume that snow and freezing weather occur in Michigan in January.

Step four: Within the system there are elements or events that are likely to increase or decrease the chances of the system's meeting its goals and objectives. These should be stated in clear language. Such elements may be gleaned from historical records of the system, other literature, and interviews with outside experts and people employed by the system.

Step five: The likelihood of occurrence of the elements identified in Step four are now stated in probabilistic terms. The variables that would increase the probability of occurrence for each event are stated. This step is similar to the requirements for constructing a cross-impact matrix as discussed in Chapter 9. But this step is carried one step further than the cross-impact matrix, in which only two elements at a time were considered. The objective here is to establish chain-like progressions of causality. One attempts to construct, over time, a chain of linkages of events; each of these events, in turn, is preceded by causally related events that would increase the probability of its occurrence. Consider this example: Social scientists frequently attribute increased gang violence to some basic moral flaw or sociopathic mentality that renders gang members incapable of any sense of social morality. Attempts to deal with gang violence usually follow treatments based on these assumptions. If we had constructed a scenario for the purposes of telling us if such treatments were working we would be hard pressed. Such attempts ignore a key element, population size, but a carefully constructed causal chain would have uncovered this: Many youth officials hope the passing of the 1956-65 baby-boom generation will result in a decline in teenage crime over the next decade. The flaw is that such general population projections do not tell us much about the specific growth rates for particular populations—in this example, the population group that provides most gang members. Gang members are drawn disproportionately from central-city, low-income minority populations, and estimates show that over the next decade the number of nonwhite males in the nation's 10-20 age group, rather than diminishing, will grow nearly 10 percent; in Los Angeles, the estimated growth is 17 percent. Thus any estimate of the success of our treatment programs must take this population growth into account.

In assigning probabilities one may be as specific as one is comfortable with the estimates, but such simple estimates as "likely (1.0), unknown (0.5), and unlikely (0.0)" appear to be useful.

From such probabilities one can make a general statement concerning the scenario and likelihood of the system's meeting its goals. That is, one can make some estimate about the best and worst worlds for the system to operate in. This is done quite simply. The probabilities assigned to the identified elements listed in Step four are summed. This gives a more or less positive net value for each scenario. A higher final score indicates a greater chance that the system will achieve its goals. In other words, the sum of the elements considered to increase the chances of the system's meeting its goals are subtracted from the sum of the elements considered to hinder the system's achieving its goals.

Step six: The attempt here is to conduct something of a sensitivity analysis so that we get some idea if our scenario model fits "reality." The scenario may likely bring to the surface images or events that have not been considered before. Such unexpected outcrops need to be reexamined by a group of experts familiar with this particular system.

Finally the scenario may reveal that some of the elements or events have a greater or lesser impact on the system than others. If this is the case then it may be necessary to assign weights to reflect the relative impact of each event. Weights will likely be of a qualitative nature but can be based on information gathered from historical literature and personal interviews. Such relationships can be expanded to include correlational analysis.

CRIMINAL JUSTICE AS A SCENARIO

This extended discussion will attempt to model the criminal justice system through the scenario technique. As noted in the beginning of this chapter, the tragic problem of crime and society's inability to cope with it are quite evident despite years of work by the criminal justice system.

The criminal justice system can be described through these behaviors and agencies: the police apprehend and arrest people suspected of breaking the law; such persons are held in custody in jails; the district attorney's office brings charges and prosecutes; private attorneys (and for those too poor, the public defender's office) provide counsel; the courts conduct trials and pass sentences; courts of appeal hear requests for a new trial and rule; prisons house those sentenced; parole officers watch those released from prison and supervise those on probation.

Very briefly, the scenario will now examine a few selected variables for their effect on criminal justice, for example, crime rates, social costs, and justice. For purposes of illustration the scenario will rely on the author's assumptions and approximated data. An actual scenario would rely much more extensively on the inputs of many experts and factual data gathered from records. Thus the outputs of the scenario stem from the hypothetical data and do not necessarily reflect an actual criminal justice system. The scenario is very interested in generating positive and negative feedback loops that actually dictate the behaviors of the system. Positive feedback loops are to be viewed as variables that enhance the occurrence of crimes while negative feedback loops decrease the commission of crimes.

The scenario will consider two (although there are many other) positive feedback influences: the low chance of getting caught while actually committing a crime, as perceived by criminals; and the long-term effect of criminals actually being back on the street in a short period of time. Likewise, the scenario will consider two negative feedback influences: quick arrest, prosecution, conviction, sentencing, and imprisonment of criminals; and citizens' defending themselves with protective postures and equipment.

Assuming a time period of one year, the scenario can now be simulated to judge the final state of the criminal justice system at the end of one year.

Consider the four feedback loops as the model is put into motion and possible subsequent effects:

The arrest rate reflects a positive relationship between number of police officers on duty, the total population, and the number of actual criminals. Since the population is increasing much faster than the number of policemen on duty, in reality this means that the individual criminal has less chance of being caught.

Increases in numbers of judges to hear cases will have several related effects; more cases are heard, more criminals are sent to prison, and there are shorter trial periods. The last effect is lessened by the tendency of lawyers to increase the trial period by raising questions concerning the constitutional rights of the individuals on trial, cause delays by raising legal technicalities, and reap financial gains from their clients through lengthy trials.

As the jails and prisons reach capacity, criminals are paroled or put on probation and released, and those awaiting trial may likely be released on their own recognizance. The effect is to put 20 to 25 percent of the actual criminal population back into the general population.

The backlog of cases in the courts causes long delays before a trial and sentencing can take place. In an effort to speed up the time to trial, the percentage of cases adjudicated by plea-bargaining (sentences are negotiated between the court and defendant through lawyers after the defendant has pleaded guilty) is increased, often resulting in a sentence of probation and the criminal goes back on the street. Also many cases involving plea-bargaining that actually involve a prison sentence usually result in a reduced term, with the actual effect being a shorter time in prison.

In criminal justice there is a nationwide trend to phase out large state prisons so that the final effect over time is a decrease in overall prison capacity. This means that in the future those criminals who normally would have gone to prison will be placed on probation. There is a high rate of recidivism, the phenomenon of repeat offenders or "hard-core criminals." As the average prison term increases, the chances of effective rehabilitation decrease.

Current data reflecting national statistics seem to indicate that quick conviction and sentencing is a strong deterrent for crime. This would seem to have a direct effect on the positive feedback loop reflecting the actual criminal's perception that he will not get caught, because it changes his view of reality. The criminal is well aware of the old adage, "Justice delayed is Justice denied."

Finally another deterrent to crime lies in the citizen's capacity to defend himself. This can take many forms, from avoiding travel at night, to better lighting in the home, to better locks.

SCENARIO CONCLUSIONS

Based on the projected effects of the four key elements or feedback loops, it would appear that our criminal justice system, as described by our scenario, is ultrastable. That is, the dynamic behavior of the system suggests that for the elements that actually tend to decrease crime there are counterforces (positive feedback loops) that tend to increase the probability of crime. The crucial concept here is the actual criminal population. If this element cannot be reduced, the criminal justice system stays in a steady state—as has actually been the case for the last decade.

The above effects are actually supported by theory in reaching our conclusion that the system is ultrastable. Weick (1969) in his provocative work, The Social Psychology of Organizing, asserts that any system with an even number of negative feedback loops is not self-correcting. The correcting mechanisms of the negative feedback loops are canceled out by the equal number of deviation-amplifying or positive feedback loops. A system with an odd number of negative feedback loops or inputs is self-correcting because it can counteract any deviations that may appear. Negative feedback loops are capable of controlling the system, because they can reverse the effects of an

earlier variable or element, but when there is an even number of negative relationships, this capability for reversing earlier effects is
canceled. To illustrate, suppose the courts send more criminals to
prison. Because the prisons soon exceed capacity they parole more
criminals. Now the criminal population actually back out on the street
has increased and consequently more crimes are committed. Naturally the police are able to make more arrests as more crimes are
committed and these criminals are returned to the courts for trial.
Since the two negative feedback loops or influences cancel each other
out, there is no control over the criminal population. The number
will increase until the system simply breaks down.

What the scenario suggests is that no single crime deterrent
policy by itself will actually have much effect on decreasing the criminal population. The system requires a policy of strategies, each
working to support the other, in order to reduce crime or to change
the dynamic characteristics of the system. Using the scenario technique, planners could identify those strategies that seem to affect
most strongly those system elements that exert more control over the
total system; in this case it would be the total criminal population at
any given time. The knowledge generated by the scenario could then
be used as a basis for action. Then fluctuations in the key system elements could be used as feedback information to measure the effects
of the various policies that were implemented.

Our scenario, with its even-numbered negative and positive
feedback loops, mirrors those difficulties found in the real world of
criminal justice planning. One variable may show improvement while
another worsens, resulting in a very stable system with no improvement in sight. But only by generating a view of what the actual system is like can any policy maker hope to implement policies that actually change the workings of the system.

SCENARIOS RECONSIDERED

Given the discussion of criminal justice through the scenario
technique, it seems worthwhile to consider additional implications
of the use of the methodology.

Scenario methodology has been criticized for not producing specific quantitative predictions—something in the form of an econometric
projection. Such criticism I think speaks more about the state of the
data than about the method per se. In fact, there is nothing intrinsic
in the method that prohibits it from being a quantitative tool. It is my
conviction, however, that our lack of knowledge about the behavior of
our social systems means that we are better off, at this time, in using
nonquantitative approaches. Too often the "precision" of a quantita-

tive method gives the false impression that the prediction is totally correct. To a policy maker such an attitude can lead to a false sense of security. We now have empirical data that demonstrate that man is not Bayesian, suggesting that the mathematical assumptions of Bayesian probabilities are invalid when applied to man. This does not mean that if we do away with conditional probabilities we should eliminate subjective probabilities. Thus the scenario can use this form of quantitative data. The main point is to remember that the mathematical aspects of scenario methodology are less important than the overall findings and events of the technique.

This is illustrated in Kahn's The Next Two Hundred Years (1976). Kahn, a physicist and mathematician by training and now director of the Hudson Institute, makes it very clear as to why he did not use highly quantitative approaches in his scenario construction. He says, "There is no assurance that more sophisticated techniques would yield better results." In simple terms, the real worth of the scenario is dependent on the events that compose it, and there are often elements in the model for which no specific data exist, yet to ignore them because of the lack of specification would be sheer folly.

Consider the criminal justice scenario. The hypothetical elements of the scenario reflect a "high-altitude" shot of the system's terrain. Such a view's purpose is to provide the planner or researcher with a whole or gestalt perspective. It provides something of an overview of the problem at hand. At this level the scenario may likely provide the user with knowledge as to whether the simple or common "folk wisdom" policy would in fact work. In our criminal justice example, we see that the quick suggestion for reducing crime—for judges to send convicted criminals to jail or prison—may actually be counterproductive, because if prisons reach capacity then a number of criminals will be paroled sooner, meaning the total criminal population is not decreased.

If the scenario user needs more details, a second scenario can be constructed using what quantitative data is available along with the insights gained from the first scenario. This can be repeated as long as details can be generated until the user now has a "ground-level" picture of the system.

Thus the scenario becomes a systematic procedure for checking out commonsense solutions through analytical and rigorous procedures. In addition, a scenario or a series of them can suggest what environments need to be created if the system is to meet its goals and objectives. The scenario can evolve to become something of a model of a system complete with predictions that can be fed into a computer for further analysis.

In analyzing any complex societal issue there is the occasional need for the policy maker to step back and take a look at the whole problem. Eventually it may even be necessary to sketch out a cross-section of the complexity in order to gain the proper perspective. The scenario's attempt to describe the whole system should reveal the major elements that largely determine the state of the system—this can be viewed as a cross-section of the realities of the system. Also such an examination may invite reexamination of how the system's elements interact that may have been overlooked. As new data are introduced into the scenario, ways in which the system accepts, rejects, or adjusts to change can be discovered.

This aspect of change leads to an important point about the use of scenarios. Too often a scenario's worth is judged by whether it predicts "right" answers. "Right," like beauty, must lie in the eye of the beholder, so no discussion of that concept will be undertaken here. But in fact the true worth of the scenario is that it allows us to see the pathways through which the system can be changed to achieve its goals. If it can tell us what needs to be done and where and the costs, then the scenario has made it possible for us to invent the future. In using the scenario one must resist the temptation to make the methodology solely an instrument of precise prediction. It is easy to become too pragmatic with the tool, thus losing sight of its theoretical power and true purpose. The focus should be on the dynamic interaction of the system's elements so that understanding is gained of how the system actually works rather than of some final predicted state. If the image of the system is to become "alive" one must learn how it in fact functions on a daily basis as when one attempts to master the workings of the human body through physiology. What is of interest is not the destination but the journey.

For those readers who have used scenario methodology, you know how difficult it is to construct a dynamic model of reality. Of course, the origin of the difficulty lies in capturing the dynamic quality of the elements. That is why the main point of scenario methodology is interaction rather than conclusion. This point is consistent with other themes in this book, mainly that the whole is greater than the sum of its parts. A scenario is much more than the mere addition of its elements. The main purpose thus becomes one of exploration and explanation; prediction is secondary. This is why even if a scenario is "wrong" (the predictions do not hold) it is in fact right because it has forced us to rethink the dynamics of the system and thereby gain the necessary insights for understanding. The argument here parallels the "no decision" versus "wrong decision" in decision-making theory. If no action (no decision) is taken there is no historical data to judge the decision. But if action is taken and it turns out to be wrong, two good results may come of it. First, corrective actions can be taken to see that the decision is corrected and made to work. Second, if the decision cannot be corrected, at least what went wrong can be discovered and precautions taken not to make the same mistake again.

Finally any consideration of the scenario methodology must note its tremendous communication capability. As in other methodologies discussed in this book, the scenario has the ability to communicate a gestalt overview of the complex problem. As a tool for logical analysis much of its power comes from its communicative ability. All assumptions and elements that go into the method are spelled out for everyone to see. The fact that everyday language rather than technical jargon is used makes the methodology comprehensible to everyone. (This aspect is totally consistent with the aims of General Systems Theory.) The reliability of the method can be measured in the sense that all scenario users can evaluate the quality of the assumptions and the relevance of the elements that compose it. The validity of the method can also be evaluated because the user is now in a position to argue that all contingencies—or the universe of necessary elements —have been considered. Thus the criteria of a reliable and valid methodology have been met.

REFERENCES

Kahn, Herman. 1976. The Next Two Hundred Years: A Scenario for America and the World. New York: William Morrow.

Weick, K. 1969. The Social Psychology of Organizing. Reading, Mass.: Addison-Wesley.

About the Author

T. HARRELL ALLEN is a professor at the University of Southern California. He was a researcher in communication systems at Battelle Memorial Institute, a research and development firm, in Columbus, Ohio. Prior to that he was an economic analyst at the Library of Congress and was a faculty member at the University of Florida.

Dr. Allen has published articles on the social sciences, human communication, organizational theory, and policy making in scholarly journals as well as in professional publications. He is the author of The Bottom Line: Communicating in the Organization.

Dr. Allen holds a Ph.D. from Ohio State University.